FAMOUS
AMERICAN
AUTHORS

By the Author

LIVES OF POOR BOYS WHO BECAME FAMOUS
LIVES OF GIRLS WHO BECAME FAMOUS
FAMOUS MEN OF SCIENCE
FAMOUS AMERICAN AUTHORS

Sarah K. Bolton

FAMOUS AMERICAN AUTHORS

REVISED BY

William A. Fahey

THOMAS Y. CROWELL COMPANY

NEW YORK

Manufactured in the United States of America
By the Vail-Ballou Press, Inc., Binghamton, New York

DESIGNED BY EDWARD A. HAMILTON

LIBRARY OF CONGRESS CATALOG CARD NO. 54-9770

Thirty-fourth Printing

EDITOR'S PREFACE

IN revising and expanding the text of *Famous American Authors*, I have been constantly aware of two significant characteristics of Sarah K. Bolton's work—simplicity and accuracy. Though she lived when the florid Victorian style was thriving, Mrs. Bolton resisted the pressures of her time and wrote with an admirable directness. The accuracy of her thumbnail biographies of the great and near great in American literature is not accidental. A woman who consulted Longfellow about the education of her son and visited socially with many of the poets and novelists about whom she wrote had first-hand information on her subjects. It is this familiarity, this sense of intimacy, that is the distinguishing charm of her writing. The book is not a collection of dry-as-dust facts culled from a library. It is a record of a woman's friendships among men and books. And with Mrs. Bolton's help, we too get to be friends with the men who wrote those books.

Of course, time, which has a way of playing tricks on those who work for the future, has necessitated some revisions. Mrs. Bolton could not have known some of the facts of Edgar Allan Poe's life, for they have only recently come to light. Nor could she have predicted the rise of his reputation as a poet. For the modern poetry that springs from his influence had not been written when Mrs. Bolton wrote her book.

Time has brought other changes, too. Great writers who were unborn in Mrs. Bolton's day have come upon the scene, made their marks and, some of them, passed away. Willa Cather, America's greatest woman novelist, has flourished since Mrs. Bolton's day. Sinclair Lewis, chronicler of Main Street and America's first Nobel Prize winner, has come and gone. Eugene O'Neill, the creator of American drama, has been at work. Carl Sandburg has

sung his song of industrial America. And Stephen Vincent Benét
has re-created our history in song and story. In presenting the
lives of these later famous American authors, I have attempted
to preserve the characteristic simplicity and accuracy of Mrs.
Bolton, while filling in the space that the passage of time had
left bare.

WILLIAM A. FAHEY

Contents

"Talent alone cannot make a writer. There must be a man behind the book."—EMERSON

"The most interesting books to me are the histories of individuals and individual minds, all autobiographies and the like. This is my favorite reading."—LONGFELLOW

Washington Irving

E VER since I have been old enough to distinguish good from evil in literary composition, your writings have been my familiar study. And, if I have done anything that deserves half the commendation you bestow on me, it is in a great measure from the study I have made of you and two or three others of the great masters of our language."

Thus wrote the historian, William H. Prescott, to Washington Irving.

The youngest of eleven children, Irving was born in the city of New York, April 3, 1783. The father, a merchant, was a Scotchman by birth, a strict Presbyterian, who lived up to the letter of the law; the mother, an English woman, the granddaughter of a clergyman, was sweet-tempered, more lenient with the children than with her husband, holding their devotion through life.

This child, born at the close of the Revolutionary War, was named for the man to whom all eyes were turned—Washington. A young Scotch maid in the family determined that the great man should see his namesake, and followed him into a shop, saying, "Please, your honor, here's a bairn was named after you."

The President put his hand upon the boy's head and gave his blessing, little thinking that in the years to come the child would give to the world, as his last and greatest work, the *Life of Washington.*

The Irving household was a merry one, though Washington used to say that, when he was young, "he was led to think, somehow or other, that everything which was pleasant was wicked." He early had a passion for books. *Robinson Crusoe, Sinbad the Sailor,* and *The World Displayed* (a collection of twenty small volumes of voyages and travels) were his especial delight. The latter he used to read under his desk at school, and, when found out by the teacher, though kindly reprimanded, was praised for his good taste in selection.

He had no love for mathematics, and frequently exchanged work with his school-fellows, they performing his examples, while he wrote their compositions. His great longing was to see the world. In his preface to the *Sketch-Book* he wrote, "How wistfully would I wander about the pier-heads in fine weather, and watch the parting ships bound to distant climes; with what longing eyes would I gaze after their lessening sails, and waft myself in imagination to the ends of the earth."

While his brothers, Peter and John, were sent to Columbia College, his education at the schools was completed before he was sixteen, a matter which he always regretted. At this age he entered a law office, and, later, that of Josiah Ogden Hoffman, a prominent lawyer, whose house became a second home to the young student.

At seventeen he made his first voyage up the Hudson River. "What a time of intense delight was that first sail through the Highlands. I sat on the deck as we slowly tided along at the foot of those stern mountains, and gazed with wonder and admiration at cliffs impending far above me, crowned with forests, with eagles sailing and screaming around them; or listened to the unseen stream dashing down precipices; or beheld rock, and tree, and cloud, and sky reflected in the glassy stream of the river."

The days were gliding by happily, but young Irving was in frail health. He coughed so badly that his best friends said, "He is not long for this world." And yet, at nineteen, scarcely able to go on with his studies, we find him writing witty articles to the *Morning Chronicle,* of which his brother Peter was the editor, signing himself "Jonathan Oldstyle." These were copied in other papers, which greatly encouraged the youth.

At twenty he made a journey with the Hoffmans to Montreal, Quebec, and Saratoga; but, his health becoming no better, at twenty-one he went to Europe, his brothers furnishing the means, "glad to add to the comfort and enjoyment of one so very near to us all."

The young man's heart turned lovingly back to his friends, for he wrote from Bordeaux, "I passed a melancholy, lonesome day, turned into my berth at night sick at heart, and lay for hours thinking of the friends I had left behind." But the sea-air proved a skilful physician.

He visited Marseilles, Genoa, Sicily, where he saw the great naval officer, Nelson; ascended Vesuvius; met Washington Allston, the painter, in Rome; enjoyed Milan; studied French for four months in Paris; and, after two years, returned to America in good health and spirits.

His love for writing drew him constantly away from the law. He soon started, with two or three friends, the humorous journal *Salmagundi,* which was sustained for a year, with a large circle of interested readers. After this he began, Peter assisting him, a *History of New York,* purporting to be written by Diedrich Knickerbocker, full of quaint humor and originality.

He was now twenty-five, a favorite in social life, with a growing literary reputation, and engaged to be married to Matilda Hoffman, daughter of the gentleman with whom he was studying. While somewhat anxious about his future, life had a richness and zest before unknown to him. And then came the shadow, which was never completely lifted till his death.

Matilda died April 26, 1809, only seventeen years old. He could never after hear her name mentioned.

After Irving's death, in a repository of which he always kept the key, a package was found marked "Private Mems." The ink was faded, and the beginning and the end of the manuscript were missing, but it was learned afterward that it had been addressed to Mrs. Foster, a warm friend, whom he had known in Berlin, as an answer to her inquiry why he had not been married. It was shown to her, with a sacred promise that no eye should see it but hers, and no copy should be taken of it.

With the faded paper was a beautiful miniature in a case, a braid of fair hair, and a slip of paper on which he had written "Matilda Hoffman." He kept through life her Bible and prayer book, under his pillow in the first days of his sorrow, and in all after years, through all his journeyings, they were his inseparable companions. And here is a portion of the story of Irving's tragic early love:

> We saw each other every day, and I became excessively attached to her. Her shyness wore off by degrees. The more I saw of her the more I had reason to admire her. Her mind seemed to unfold leaf by leaf, and every time to discover new sweetness. Nobody knew her so well as I, for she was generally timid and silent; but I in a manner studied her excellence.

Never did I meet with more intuitive rectitude of mind, more native delicacy, more exquisite propriety in word, thought, and action, than in this young creature. I am not exaggerating; what I say was acknowledged by all who knew her. Her brilliant little sister used to say that people began by admiring her, but ended by loving Matilda. For my part, I idolized her. I felt at times rebuked by her superior delicacy and purity, and as if I was a coarse, unworthy being in comparison. . . . In the midst of this struggle and anxiety, Matilda was taken ill with a cold. Nothing was thought of it at first; but she rapidly grew worse, and fell into a consumption. I cannot tell you what I suffered. The ills that I have undergone in this life have been dealt out to me drop by drop, and I have tasted all their bitterness. I saw her fade rapidly away; beautiful, and more beautiful, and more angelical to the last. I was often by her bedside; and in her wandering state of mind she would talk to me with a sweet, natural, and affecting eloquence, that was overpowering. I saw more of the beauty of her mind in that delirious state than I had ever known before. Her malady was rapid in its career, and hurried her off in two months. Her dying struggles were painful and protracted. For three days and nights I did not leave the house, and scarcely slept. I was by her when she died; all the family were assembled round her, some praying, others weeping, for she was adored by them all. I was the last one she looked upon.

I cannot tell you what a horrid state of mind I was in for a long time. I seemed to care for nothing; the world was a blank to me. I abandoned all thoughts of the law. I went into the country, but could not bear solitude, yet could not endure society. There was a dismal horror continually in my mind, that made me fear to be alone. I had often to get up in the night, and seek the bedroom of my brother, as if the having a human being by me would relieve me from the frightful gloom of my own thoughts.

Months elapsed before my mind would resume any tone. . . . I seemed to drift about without aim or object, at the mercy of every breeze; my heart wanted anchorage. I was naturally susceptible, and tried to form other attachments, but my heart would not hold on; it would continually recur to what it had lost; and whenever there was a pause in the hurry of novelty and excitement, I would sink into dismal dejection. For years I could not talk on the subject of this hopeless regret; I could not even mention her name; but her image was continually before me, and I dreamt of her incessantly.

Who does not recall the *Rural Funerals* of the *Sketch-Book*, where "the love which survives the tomb is one of the noblest attributes of the soul"; or *St. Mark's Eve*, in *Bracebridge Hall*, where Irving said, "There are departed beings that I have loved as I never shall love again in this world—that have loved me as I never again shall be loved."

Finally, the broken thread of life was tied again, and the *History of New York* was finished, but ever after the writings were to have a deeper note, a more tender touch and grace.

For this book, which, Charles Dudley Warner says, "in spontaneity, freshness, breadth of conception, and joyous vigor, belongs to the springtime of literature," Irving received three thousand dollars. After spending some time in Washington to look after the business interests of his brother Peter, he undertook in 1812 the editorship of the *Analectic Magazine*, at a salary of fifteen hundred dollars; but periodical labor was irksome to him, and criticism of books especially distasteful, for he wished to be just and yet could not bear to be severe, and therefore withdrew from the enterprise.

After serving for a time upon the staff of the Governor of New York, he decided to visit Europe and assist Peter, who was in business in Liverpool. Financial troubles came to many in consequence of the War of 1812, and to the Irving brothers among the rest. After many months of care,—"I would not again experience the anxious days and sleepless nights which have been my lot since I have taken hold of business to possess the wealth of Crœsus," said Washington Irving,—the brothers failed, and went into bankruptcy. It was a humiliating ordeal for two proud-spirited men, and for some time Washington shut himself out from society and studied German night and day to keep out uncomfortable thoughts. The disaster was perhaps the one thing necessary to force him to his pen for his support; nevertheless, the losses and debts were well-nigh killing to a man of honor.

The death of his mother at this time rendered it unnecessary for him to return to America, as he had expected, and he went up to London, determined to earn his living by writing. He could scarcely force himself to work, so depressed was he.

Soon thereafter came a gleam of sunshine in the clouds. From his brother William, who was in Congress, he received the intelligence that a clerkship in the Navy Department was open to him, at a salary of twenty-four hundred dollars; but he had decided, once for all, to try literature, and he declined the offer, much to the surprise and disappointment of his brothers.

So disturbed was Washington by the certainty of their displeasure, and the uncertainty of remuneration from writing, that for two months he could scarcely pen a line.

He was now thirty-six. Under such leaden skies, the *Sketch-Book* had been written and sent to America to find a publisher. The first volume contained *The Voyage, Roscoe, The Wife,* and *Rip Van Winkle;* the second, *English Writers on America, Rural Life in England, The Broken Heart,* and the *Art of Book-Making.*

Both little volumes met with a hearty reception. Twenty years later, Chambers' *Cyclopedia of English Literature,* said:

"*Rip Van Winkle* and *Sleepy Hollow* are perhaps the finest pieces of original fictitious writing that this century has produced, next to the works of Scott."

The Broken Heart, the lady mentioned being the daughter of the noted Irish barrister, Curran, was especially liked. Byron said, "That is one of the finest things ever written on earth. Irving is a genius; and he has something better than genius,—a heart. He never wrote that without weeping; nor can I hear it without tears. I have not wept much in this world, for trouble never brings tears to my eyes; but I always have tears for *The Broken Heart.*"

When the words of praise came back from New York, Irving wrote his friends, "I feel almost appalled by such success, and fearful that it cannot be real, or that it is not fully merited, or that I shall not act up to the expectations that may be formed. . . . I have felt cast down, blighted, and broken-spirited, and these sudden rays of sunshine agitate even more than they revive me."

As it was rumored that some person was about to publish the *Sketch-Book* in London, Irving thought it best to send the work to Murray, a prominent publisher, and it was "declined with thanks," a quotation well-known to unknown authors.

What should be done? He bethought himself of Walter Scott, who had in prosperous days invited him to Abbotsford, and of whom Irving said, "Everything that comes within his influence seems to catch a beam of that sunshine that plays round his heart."

At once Scott wrote asking if he would become editor of a magazine, at twenty-five hundred dollars a year (which he declined) and offering any aid possible. Meantime, Irving had brought out the book at his own risk, his publisher had failed, and now the noble-hearted Scott helped him "out of the mire," as he said, by prevailing upon Murray to publish the book, and pay one thousand dollars for the copyright. He never ceased to be grateful for this kindness, and for that of Lockhart, Scott's son-in-law, who kindly reviewed the book in *Blackwood's Magazine.*

Life was growing brighter. So well had the *Sketch-Book* succeeded, that Murray had sent him an extra thousand dollars, and written him, "I am convinced I did not half know you, and, esteeming you highly as I did, certainly my esteem is doubled by my better knowledge of you." Publishers are human, and success influences them as it does other mortals.

In 1820, when he was thirty-seven, he visited Paris again, meeting Canning, Sir Sydney Smith, Thomas Moore, the Irish poet, and Bancroft, who had been two years at Göttingen. Here he wrote industriously on *Bracebridge Hall.*

On his return to London he brought with him, for publication, some plays of John Howard Payne, author of *Home, Sweet Home,* whose debts, by unfortunate business matters, prevented his remaining in England. To the end of his life, Irving was always helping writers as Walter Scott had helped him.

Visiting his sister in Birmingham, he became ill for four months, from lack of exercise and confining himself too closely within doors. When restored to health, he sent *Bracebridge Hall* to America for publication, stipulating that it be given to a certain publisher, who, though he had failed, "is one who showed a disposition to serve me, and who did serve me in the time of my necessity, and I should despise myself could I for a moment forget it."

The book was published May 21, 1822, in America, and two days later in London, Murray giving him five thousand dollars for the copyright. This showed plainly that he had not been unwise in declining the clerkship in the Navy.

Needing rest and change, he went to Germany; ascended the Rhine to Wiesbaden, thence to Mayence, beginning his *Tales of a Traveller;* then to Munich and Salzburg, "one of the most romantic places, as to its situation and scenery, he had ever beheld,"—who that has ever been there can forget it?—spending a month in Vienna, and then several months with the Fosters, in Dresden, studying French, Italian, and German.

After Irving's death one of the daughters of Mrs. Foster wrote of him, "He was thoroughly a gentleman, not merely externally in manners and look, but to the innermost fibres and core of his heart. Sweet-tempered, gentle, fastidious, sensitive, and gifted with the warmest affections, the most delightful and invariably interesting companion, gay and full of humor, even in spite of occasional fits of melancholy, which he was, however, seldom subject to when with those he liked —a gift of conversation that flowed like a full river in sunshine, bright, easy, and abundant."

Finally he returned to Paris, working fitfully on his *Tales of a Traveller,* sometimes "twenty-eight pages a day—clean and neat writing," sometimes tired, sleepless, and inactive. At last the book was ready, and Murray gave him seven thousand five hundred dollars for the two volumes.

With this prosperity there was a sense of unrest often in his heart. He wrote to a friend, "I think I was formed for an honest, domestic, uxorious man, and I cannot hear of my old cronies snugly nestled down with good wives and fine children round them, but I feel for the moment desolate and forlorn. What a haphazard, schemeless life mine has been, that here I should be, at this time of life, scribbling month after month, and year after year, far from home, without any means or prospect of entering into matrimony, which I abso-

lutely believe indispensable to the happiness and even comfort of the after part of existence."

In 1826, when he was forty-three, A. H. Everett, our minister to Madrid, with whom he was acquainted, suggested to
him that he translate *Navarrete's Voyages of Columbus,* soon
to appear. Accordingly, he went to Spain, and soon made
up his mind that, with the rich material at hand, he could
write a *Life of Columbus* which would be more interesting
work than translating.

He at once began in earnest, sometimes writing all day
and until twelve at night. After a year and a half, "the hardest
application and toil of the pen" he had ever seen, yet the most
satisfactory, the *Life* was finished, and the copyright sold to
Murray for fifteen thousand dollars. The manuscript was
also leased to a Philadelphia firm for seven years, for six hundred dollars each year, and for a second edition and an
"abridgment" he received from America six thousand dollars.
This abridgment he wrote in nineteen days, giving it to Murray without charge, who sold ten thousand copies of it for his
Family Library.

He had now, as he said, "a moderate hope as to the future.
. . . The literary success of the *History of Columbus* has been
greater than I anticipated, and gives me hopes that I have
executed something which may have greater duration than
I anticipate for my works of mere imagination."

Deeply interested now in all that pertained to the history
of Spain, *The Conquest of Granada* began to shape itself in
his mind. He repaired to Seville for a year, and worked ear-
nestly. When the work was completed, it was sold in America
for nearly five thousand dollars, and to Murray for ten thousand.

So delighted were the people of Spain that they gave him

the diploma of the Royal Academy of History. He had come to fame now, and fortune. He wrote to Peter, "I feel anxious to make the most of my present sunshine; but the very anxiety agitates me, and I feel at times a little perplexed what to take hold of."

But he soon decided to work on the *Alhambra* and the old exquisite Moorish palace became his home. "I take my breakfast in the saloon of the ambassadors or the court of the Lions," he wrote to his friends; "and in the evening, when I throw by my pen, I wander about the old palace until quite late, with nothing but bats and owls to keep me company. . . . I have nothing but the sound of water, the humming of bees, and the singing of nightingales to interrupt the profound silence of my abode."

The touching history of the Moors found response in Irving's heart, and the exquisite beauty of their workmanship found expression in his distinguished prose.

After three years in Spain, to his great surprise, he was appointed Secretary of Legation at London, which position he accepted, more to please his friends than himself, and bade good-by to the Alhambra, where he had lived in a "kind of Oriental dream."

On his forty-seventh birthday, the Royal Society of Literature voted him one of their fifty-guinea gold medals. In less than a month, Oxford University gave him the degree of Doctor of Laws, an honor which he appreciated, though he never used the title. He had worked hard, and had been rewarded. After two years he resigned his position, and arranged for the publication of the *Alhambra* for six thousand dollars in Europe, and three thousand in America.

He had long been eager to return to his native land, and on April 11, 1832, he set sail for New York, arriving after forty days. He had gone away scarcely more than a boy. Now, after seventeen years, he had come back at the flood tide of fame and honor. He was overwhelmed with courtesies from his proud countrymen. A public dinner was given him in New York, presided over by the President of Columbia College. When Irving said in his address, "I am asked how long I mean to remain here. They know but little of my heart or my feelings who can ask me this question. I answer, As long as I live," —three cheers were given again and again, and handkerchiefs were waved on every side. From natural shyness he declined receptions in Philadelphia, Baltimore, and elsewhere.

Late in the autumn, Irving made an extended tour through the West, finding Ohio "a perfect garden-spot," and spent some weeks among the Indian tribes. From this trip came the *Tour on the Prairies*, for which he received about five thousand dollars.

Irving had always longed for a home. It was natural that he should seek it upon the Hudson, which he had so much loved in early youth. At Tarrytown, not far from the spot where Ichabod Crane met the Headless Horseman in *The Legend of Sleepy Hollow*, Irving purchased a stone cottage, with about fifteen acres of ground. There, together with his brothers John and Ebenezer, and the five daughters of the latter, he made his beloved "Sunnyside." "Old bachelor though I be," he used to say, "I cannot do without womankind about me," and the nieces were to him like daughters.

In 1836, in connection with his nephew, Pierre, he wrote, at the request of John Jacob Astor, the history of a colony founded at the mouth of the Columbia River, in Oregon, and this book, *Astoria*, had a large sale.

Irving had now been at work for three months on the *History of the Conquest of Mexico*, when he found that Prescott had already sent fifteen hundred dollars to Madrid for books and manuscripts on the same subject. Though it was a great sacrifice, he at once wrote to Prescott, saying, "In yielding up the theme to you, I feel that I am but doing my duty in leaving one of the most magnificent themes in American history to be treated by one who will build up from it an enduring monument in the literature of our country."

Having suffered considerable losses in Western investments, Irving was still dependent upon his pen. Years before, he had been asked by a publisher to write the *Life of Washington,* and he now set himself to this work, when, to his amazement, Daniel Webster, who was then Secretary of State, sponsored his appointment as Minister to Spain. He considered it the "crowning honor of his life," though he could hardly bear to leave his home.

He reached London in 1842, where he received every attention, and also at Madrid. Here for three years he lived, and served his government faithfully. Webster used to say that he always laid aside all other correspondence to read a diplomatic despatch from Irving.

When he was sixty-two he wrote to friends in America, "My heart yearns for home; and as I have now probably turned the last corner in life, and my remaining years are growing scanty in number, I begrudge every one that I am obliged to pass separated from my cottage and my kindred. . . . I think, of late years, living at home, with those around to love and cherish me, my heart has become accustomed to look around for others to lean upon."

He was happy to be back at Sunnyside in the autumn of 1846, and soon began work again on his *Life of Washington.* An arrangement was now made with Mr. Putnam, the publisher to bring out Irving's complete works, on which the author obtained a royalty of nine thousand dollars yearly for about eight years. At this time he also received over ten thousand dollars as one of the executors of the Astor estate.

Two other books now came from his pen—a charming *Life of Goldsmith,* written in two months, and two volumes of *Mahomet and His Successors,* for which he had obtained the materials in Spain.

And then, at sixty-seven, he went eagerly to his *Life of Washington.* "If I can only live to finish it," he said, "I would be willing to die the next moment. If I only had ten years more of life! I never felt more able to write. I might not conceive as I did in earlier days, when I had more romance of feeling; but I could execute with more rapidity and freedom."

The first volume was published the following year (1855); this year also he gathered some of his miscellaneous writings into a volume called *Wolfert's Roost,* which had a large sale. The fourth volume was published when he was seventy-four. The fifth and last volume was written with much physical suffering. Sleeplessness developed from his habit of reading and writing late at night; prostration of the nervous system followed. He had always been somewhat subject to moods and caprices in writing. "These periods of the heat and glow of composition," he said, "have been the happiest hours of my life. I have never found in anything outside of the four walls of my study any enjoyment equal to sitting at my writing-desk, with a clean page, a new theme, and a mind wide-awake."

When the fifth book was finished, he said to his nephew, "I am getting ready to go; I am shutting up my doors and windows."

On the 28th of November, 1859, upon retiring for the night, Irving said to his niece, "Well, I must arrange my pillows for another weary night! If this could only end!" when, suddenly, he pressed his hand to his left side, and fell lifeless upon the floor.

When the news of his death reached New York, flags were

hung at half-mast, and when he was buried, at sunset, December 1, in the little cemetery near "Sleepy Hollow,"—next to his mother, as he had wished—the bells of his native city tolled for their honored dead.

Of Irving it could be said, "There was a man behind the books." Genial, kind, and helpful, he overcame poverty, ill-health, sorrow, and, with a steadfast purpose, won the victory in his life.

James Fenimore Cooper

IN the days gone by, James Fenimore Cooper was known to every lad, and so he should be now, but unfortunately in many libraries the works of others are crowding the work of the pioneer into the background. He is just as interesting today as when our fathers and grandfathers hung spellbound over his pages. Some of his work will endure, and though he was our first American novelist, he is still in some ways one of the greatest. His work has been more widely read, translated into more languages, and published in more literary centers than those of almost any other writer of his country. He was the pioneer in three of the greatest fields of fiction—that of the open as found in forest and prairie, the salty romance of the high seas, and the American historical novel.

He had many followers, but few of them have succeeded in painting nature as he has. His women were mostly the flimsiest kind of uninteresting creatures, made up, as he said, of "religious and female decorum." But he was an excellent "story-teller," and his books are full of the most interesting and exciting events imaginable. His novels blaze with action from start to finish. Not even the pulp adventure thrillers can get their heroes into and out of more scrapes than Cooper arranged for his characters.

Up to the age of thirty-one Cooper probably never even thought of writing a book. He was born in Burlington, New Jersey, in 1789. His father soon afterward moved to New York State, where he had a tract of some 17,000 acres. He built for himself a home on the shores of Otsego Lake, and later the village of Cooperstown grew up around his stately mansion. Here in the primeval forest young Fenimore roamed at will. In the contest between advancing civilization and the pursuits of the squatter, he acquired that intimate knowledge of forest life which he later portrayed so truthfully in his *Leather-Stocking Tales*. At the age of thirteen he was sent to Yale, but he got into some frolic and was dismissed in disgrace in his third year. He longed to go to sea, and shipped before the mast as a common sailor for one year. Then he was made a midshipman in the United States Navy, and for five years he cruised about, making himself master of that knowledge and detail of nautical life which he afterward employed to so much advantage in his sea tales.

Cooper was married to a Miss Delancey in 1811, and retired from the Navy. For a few years they lived happily in Westchester County, a locality afterward made famous in *The Spy*. Then Cooper's father died, and the son took possession of the family mansion at Cooperstown and settled down to the quiet life of the country gentleman. He was very fond of reading, and often read aloud to his wife. One day, having finished reading an English novel, he threw it down with impatience, exclaiming: "I could write a better story than that myself!" His wife laughed incredulously, but encouraged him to try. He did try, and the result was so successful that in 1820 he anonymously published a book entitled *Precaution*. At that time no one had thought of writing a novel with the scene laid in America, and Cooper followed in the footsteps of others. *Precaution* was so English in its setting that no one had a suspicion of its American authorship. The success which it met was not great, but Cooper realized that, as he had not failed with a novel describing British life, of which he knew little, he might succeed with one on American life, of which he was so well informed.

Scott's *Ivanhoe* was just then taking the public by storm, and Cooper at once formed the plan of writing an American historical novel. So he set to work upon *The Spy,* which appeared in 1821. It was a tale of the Revolution, and Harvey Birch, the spy, is one of the most interesting and impressive characters in romantic literature. The book was an instant success. Cooper was at once hoisted to fame, and called "The American Scott," a title which he did not much relish. The book ran through edition after edition in this country, and was translated into four languages.

Cooper was so pleased with the praise that came to him from both sides of the Atlantic that he determined to write another book, declaring that America was alive with material. He accordingly turned to the backwoods and the scenes of frontier life. Here Cooper was in his element, on ground familiar to him from infancy, but his book, *The Pioneers,* was a revelation to the outside world. It was in this work that one of the grandest characters in fiction, the brave, true, simple-hearted old backwoodsman, Natty Bumppo, the famous Leather-Stocking, first appeared. He gave his name to a series of tales which occupied the author about twenty years; but, strange to say, they were not written in regular order. To follow the story logically, one should read first *The Deerslayer,* next *The Last of the Mohicans,* followed by *The*

Pathfinder, then *The Pioneers,* and, last of all, *The Prairie,* in which the death of Leather-Stocking occurs.

Sir Walter Scott's *Pirate* appeared in 1821, and Cooper, who seems to have been jealous of Scott's popularity, declared at once that it could not have been written by a man familiar with the sea. To prove it, he wrote *The Pilot,* which was immediately stamped everywhere as a genuine salt-water novel, and at the present time it is still one of the best of its kind. It told again the thrilling exploits of John Paul Jones. The great hero, Long Tom Coffin, is the only one of Cooper's characters fitted to stand beside the famous Leather-Stocking, although Harvey Birch, the versatile peddler-spy, is unlikely to pass into oblivion.

Cooper wrote thirty-two novels in all, and fully demonstrated that he was as much at home in the deep forest as in the wide plain or upon the sea. He considered *The Pathfinder* and *The Deerslayer* his best works, and many of his critics agree with him. In addition to his novels, Cooper published *Sketches of Switzerland, Gleanings in Europe, History of the Navy of the United States, Lives of Distinguished Naval Officers,* etc. Though much of what he wrote was intended for boys and young people, Cooper was himself very unpopular among the young who knew him. In fact, he was always engaged in a quarrel with the boys of his town. They despised him and never lost a chance to torment him. It is said that on a few occasions they even went so far as to stone and rotten-egg him.

After the publication of *The Spy,* Cooper went to New York City, where he lived the better part of the four years following. Here he made many friends, in spite of the fact that he was very contentious and prone to heated discussions. In 1826 he made ready for a sojourn in Europe, and before his departure was tendered a dinner in New York which was attended by many of the most prominent men of the nation.

Abroad, he enjoyed the respect of the great literary personages. Blaisdell, in speaking of this time, says: "It would be interesting to tell how Sir Walter Scott sought him out in Paris and renewed the acquaintance again in London; how he lived in friendship and intimacy with General Lafayette at the French capital; to tell of his association with Wordsworth and Rogers in London; his intimate friendship with the great sculptor, Greenough, and his fondness for Italy, which country he preferred to all others outside of America; of the delightful little villa where he lived in Florence, where he said he could look out upon green leaves and write to the music of the birds; to picture him settled for a summer in Naples; living in Tasso's villa at Sorrento, writing his stories in the same house in which the great Italian author had lived, with the same glorious view of the sea and bay and the surf dashing almost against its walls."

Cooper was much annoyed by the ignorance and prejudice of the English in all that related to his country. It is said that at literary meetings and dinner parties in London he always carried in his pockets volumes from such poets as Bryant and Halleck, from which he often read quotations, to prove his assertion of the merits of American poets and writers.

After his return to Cooperstown, in 1833, Cooper lost much of his popularity because of his caustic pen, which was prone to flay everyone who did not come up to his ideas of patriotism, or failed to walk the chalk-marks of high-minded, high-principled refinement which he drew. W. C. Bryant says of him: "James Fenimore Cooper was certainly the most remarkable personage in the whole list of American men of letters. His character was noble and grand and his personality, to those who knew him intimately, genial and lovable. But his temper was irritable to a degree almost unparalleled, and his judgment as to matters of conduct often downright absurd. His history (especially the years of his life after his return from Europe when he was involved with the people of Cooperstown over land disputes, and with editors all over the country in libel suits) is a sad one. It shows a magnificent endowment of ability and character largely frittered away in courses of action that a sane man would never have dreamed of. His splendid powers for months and years were devoted to controversies and legal disputes that should never have been thought of, and his work, of which he accomplished so much, can show the hall-mark of his genius in only a few volumes." It is said that the editors of New York stood in wholesome fear of him, and styled him "The Great Prosecutor," because he brought so many libel suits against them.

However stormy Cooper's public life may have been, his domestic life was exceedingly happy. He was blessed with rugged health until the latter part of his life, when he was a victim of dropsy. His last illness was of only a few days' duration, and to the end his vigorous intellect remained unimpaired. He died on September 14, 1851, one day before the sixty-second anniversary of his birth. He was laid to rest in the cemetery at Cooperstown. His dearly loved wife, who had come to him forty years before as a bride of nineteen, followed him only four months later. Their graves are now marked by a marble statue of Leather-Stocking, with his dog and gun.

A few days after Cooper's death memorial services were held in New York City. Prominent men from all over the country assembled to do honor to their distinguished countryman; Washington Irving presided, and William Cullen Bryant delivered a fitting tribute to him who had been the first to show

how fit for fiction were the scenes, the characters, and the history of his native land. Over one hundred years have passed since then, but Cooper's men of the sea and his men of the forest and the plain not only survive, but remain today among the best of their kind.

William Cullen Bryant

Bryant's writings transport us into the depths of the solemn primeval forest, to the shores of the lonely lake, the banks of the wild nameless stream, on the brow of the rocky upland rising like a promontory from amidst a wide ocean of foliage; while they shed around us the glories of a climate fierce in its extremes, but splendid in all its vicissitudes.—WASHINGTON IRVING

THE name of William Cullen Bryant brings to the reader's mind a vision of deep woods, or the silence of solitary places. Like Wordsworth, his nearest English parallel, he was in intimate harmony with nature. Yet during the greater part of his life, Bryant was a city dweller. His birthplace and early home, however, was in the country, and some of his most famous poems were written long before he had reached manhood.

William Cullen Bryant, the second in a family of seven children, was born on November 3, 1794. His father practiced medicine in the little village of Cummington, Mass., following in the footsteps of a father and grandfather who had also been physicians, and were descended from *Mayflower* stock. Dr. Bryant was very fond of books and well-read in his profession. He knew several languages and delighted in poetry and music. His son William owed a great deal to his help and guidance, and ever cherished a most tender memory of him whose life was "marked with some act of goodness every day." He tells us about him in several of his poems. In *The Ages* he says:

> Peace to the just man's memory,—let it grow
>   Greener with years, and blossom through the flight
> Of ages; let the mimic canvas show
>   His calm benevolent features; let the light
>   Stream on his deeds of love, that shunned the sight
> Of all but heaven, and, in the book of fame,
>   The glorious record of his virtues write,
> And hold it up to men, and bid them claim
> A palm like his, and catch from him the hallowed flame.

Bryant's mother was Sarah Snell, a descendant of John Alden and Priscilla, from whom Longfellow was also descended. She was a woman of character and domestic virtue, and Byrant loved to describe her as a housewife fashioned on the old Hebrew model, such as is pictured in the thirty-first Proverb:

> The heart of her husband doth safely trust in her. She will do him good and not evil all the days of her life.
> She seeketh wool and flax and worketh diligently with her hands.
> She looketh well to the ways of her household, and eateth not the bread of idleness.
> Her children arise up and call her blessed; her husband also, and he praiseth her.

William Cullen from the very first was a bright child. He could run alone before he was a year old, and knew all his letters at the age of sixteen months. He began to make rhymes at an early age. When he was ten years old his grandfather gave him a ninepenny coin for making a rhymed version of the first chapter of the book of Job. The same year he wrote, and recited at the school exhibition, a poem describing the school. His teacher was so proud of it that he had it printed in the county paper. There was nothing very remarkable in these early poems, except the correctness of rhyme and measure.

Very early in life Bryant began to hope that he might be a poet, and he wove this petition into the daily prayers which his mother and grandmother taught him. His father saw the lad's budding genius, and did all he could to encourage him. The Bryants had a fairly good library, and young Cullen, as he was called at home, read every scrap of poetry that came in his way. Then, too, his surroundings were ideal for the fostering of a poet. The little hamlet lying on the banks of the clear mountain rivulet, the quiet old mountains, beautiful valleys, restful groves, and noisy streams all woke a song of Nature in the young poet's heart that warbled till his last pulse beat. Though over half a century of his busy life was spent in New York City, the din and uproar of his surroundings never drowned the voice of Nature or quenched his longing for his native hills. Ever the haunts of boyhood were the best, though he traveled much and far, crossing the ocean six times.

> It is sweet
> To linger here among the flitting birds
> And leaping squirrels, wandering brooks, and winds,
> That shake the leaves and scatter as they pass,
> A fragrance from the cedars, thickly set
> With pale blue berries. In these peaceful shades—
> Peaceful, unpruned, immeasurably old—

My thoughts go up the long dim path of years,
Back to the earliest days of liberty.

Bryant had very little formal education. He attended the village school, studied Latin with his uncle, had a few months of Greek and mathematics with a neighboring minister, and one year in Williams College. He longed to go to Yale, but Dr. Bryant could not afford to send him. So Cullen went home, determined to have a good education, even if he could not continue at college. He read all the books in his father's medical library, and barely escaped being a physician. He performed many of the experiments the books suggested and thus got a good knowledge of chemistry. He studied botany. He went into the dead languages with vim, and he read everything he could lay his hands on, especially the poetry of Burns, Cowper, Thompson, Wordsworth, and Southey.

While carrying on these studies he helped with the farm work. But there were four brothers, all stronger than he, and it was plain that he was not needed at home. He must seek elsewhere. What should he do? His heart leaned toward literature, but in those days writing was a very poor occupation indeed. He could not hope to earn a living with his pen, so he turned his mind to law, and at the age of seventeen entered a law office in Worthington, a little village some four or five miles from his home.

It has been said that, "A young man's first year's study of the law commonly affects him like his first cigar, or his first year before the mast." And this was the way it agreed with Cullen. He did not like it at all, and said his only enjoyment was when he could smuggle in Irving or Wordsworth instead of Blackstone. He was terribly homesick, and begged his father to be allowed to go to Boston. But Dr. Bryant said the expenses would be too heavy, and that he could not afford it without doing injustice to his younger boys. Of course, Cullen did not wish to rise at the expense of his brothers, so they compromised and he went to Bridgewater, a larger place than Worthington, which Cullen was wont to describe scornfully as "a cow stable and a blacksmith shop." Here he lived with his grandfather, and studied law with Mr. Bayliss, a well-known lawyer of the times. Young Bryant was admitted to the bar at the age of twenty-one. It was a proud day for him when he walked into the library at home, with his license in his pocket, and sat down to a family counsel as to where he should "settle." He wanted to go to Boston, but his father talked him out of the notion, and advised Plainfield, a little village lying in full view from the window, though distant five or six miles. The chances for legal services here might not be great, but on the other hand the expenses would be light.

That evening the young man set out on foot over the hills to arrange for "hanging out his shingle." This trip had results which posterity would long remember. As he trudged along, feeling very forlorn and desolate, the sun sank in a bank of rosy splendor which evoked all his poet's rapture. He stood gazing in rapt wonder till a solitary bird rose up and made its way along the illuminated horizon. The lone wanderer inspired him with new strength and courage. He watched it out of sight. That night on going to his room he penned the lines which many people have said they would wish to keep if all but one of Bryant's poems were to be destroyed forever. Here they are:

LINES TO A WATERFOWL

Whither, 'midst falling dew,
While glow the heavens with the last steps of day,
Far, through their rosy depths, dost thou pursue
    Thy solitary way?

Vainly the fowler's eye
Might mark thy distant flight to do thee wrong,
As, darkly painted on the crimson sky,
  Thy figure floats along.

Seek'st thou the plashy brink
Of weedy lake, or marge of river wide,
Or where the rocking billows rise and sink
  On the chafed ocean side?

There is a power whose care
Teaches thy way along that pathless coast,
The desert and illimitable air—
  Lone wandering, but not lost.

All day thy wings have fanned,
At that far height, the cold thin atmosphere,
Yet stoop not, weary, to the welcome land,
  Though the dark night is near.

And soon that toil shall end;
Soon shalt thou find a summer home, and rest,
And scream among thy fellows; reeds shall bend,
  Soon, o'er thy sheltered nest.

Thou'rt gone, the abyss of heaven
Hath swallowed up thy form; yet, on my heart
Deeply hath sunk the lesson thou hast given,
  And shall not soon depart.

He who, from zone to zone,
Guides through the boundless sky thy certain flight,
In the long way that I must tread alone
  Will lead my steps aright.

These lines, however, did not see the light of print until
some three or four years later. Bryant tucked them away with
other poems, which are now famous, and sought eagerly for

clients. But Plainfield was a peaceable community and had little need for lawyers, so that in about eight months he was glad to accept a proposition to enter partnership with a young lawyer at Great Barrington. He was greatly pleased with his new location on the gently flowing Housatonic, and it was characteristic of his poet's soul that he should write in glowing terms of the smooth green meadow, the murmuring waters, the craggy hills, and the many-colored forest, and say nothing at all of the industrial and commercial activities around him whence his living was to come. His eye was more intent upon material for verse making than for opportunities of writing briefs. And he could not keep from putting these impressions into rhyme, but he had long since gotten over the habit of reading his verses to his father, and he seemed unable to measure their true worth himself, for he continued to store them away. Many of the verses written at this time show his unrest. In *Green River* he tells us:—

> That fairy music I never hear,
> Nor gaze on those waters so sweet and clear,
> And mark them winding away from sight,
> Darkened with shade or flashing with light,
> While o'er them the vine to its thicket clings,
> And the zephyr stoops to freshen his wings,
> But I wish that Fate had left me free
> To wander these quiet haunts with thee,
> Till the eating cares of earth should depart,
> And the peace of the scene pass into my heart;
> But I envy thy stream, as it glides along,
> Through its beautiful banks, in a trance of song.

It was Dr. Bryant who opened the eyes of the world to his son's genius. One day, while rummaging through an old dark desk which Cullen used when at home, he came upon the manuscript verses of *Thanatopsis* and *An Inscription Upon the Entrance to a Wood*. His eyes filled with tears, and he was so certain of their greatness that he set out at once for Boston and gave them into the hands of his friend Phillips, editor of *The North American Review.* Phillips was delighted, but he thought the fond father was in some way mistaken. "No one on this side of the Atlantic is capable of writing such verses," he said. But Dr. Bryant succeeded in convincing him, and he published the poems. "They soon found their way into the school books of the country. They were quoted from the pulpit and upon the hustings. Their gifted author had a national fame before he had a vote, and in due time *Thanatopsis* took the place which it still retains among the masterpieces of poetry."

The first great trial of Bryant's life came to him in the early death of his father, his best counselor and friend. But Providence sent him compensation in the shape of Fanny Fairchild, the recently orphaned daughter of a well-to-do farmer on Green River. She became the inspiration of many of his best poems. He speaks of her in *A Summer Ramble, The Future Life, The Snow Shower, The Life That Is, May Evening, A Lifetime,* and others. They were married June 11, 1821. Hear what he says of her in *Oh Fairest of the Rural Maids:*

> The twilight of the trees and rocks
> Is in the light shade of thy locks;
> Thy step is as the wind, that weaves
> Its playful way among the leaves.
>
> Thy eyes are springs, in whose serene
> And silent waters heaven is seen;
> Their lashes are the herbs that look
> On their young figures in the brook.
>
> The forest depths by foot unpressed,
> Are not more sinless than thy breast;
> The holy peace that fills the air
> Of those calm solitudes is there.

The year following his marriage, Bryant was asked to make the poetic address before the Phi Beta Kappa Society of Harvard College. He gave them *The Ages,* and everywhere it was spoken of as the finest poem ever given before the society. People thought it very remarkable work for a young man and he was asked to publish his poems in a volume. The result was a little book of eight poems, and it is said that if he had never written another line he would still have held a lasting place among the poets of America. The poems in his first book were: *The Ages, To a Waterfowl, Fragment from Simonides, An Inscription Upon the Entrance to a Wood, The Yellow Violet, The Song, Green River,* and *Thanatopsis.*

Bryant's visit to Boston and Cambridge made him dislike his profession and the society of Great Barrington more than ever. Friends began to urge him to come to New York and take up literature for his life work. Finally in the spring of 1824 he went up on a prospecting tour, and everything possible was done to make the place inviting to him. But Bryant could not bring himself to drop law, in which he knew he could make a living, for the more agreeable profession of literature, in which he felt he would probably bring himself and family to the verge of starvation, so decided to stick to Great Barrington a while longer.

Soon came a blow which cast another shadow on his native hills. His sister, the beloved companion of his boyhood days, followed her father into a consumptive's grave. Bryant erected for her that beautiful monument of verse called *The Death of the Flowers:*

In the cold moist earth we laid her, when the forest cast the leaf,
And we wept that one so lovely should have a life so brief:
Yet not unmeet it was that one, like that young friend of ours,
So gentle and so beautiful, should perish with the flowers.

It is interesting to know that the poet received only $2 for this beautiful poem. Fifty years later any publisher in the land would gladly have paid him one hundred times that amount.

In 1825 Bryant was offered a place on the editorial staff of *The New York Review* at a salary of $1000 per year, and he accepted gladly, for the sum was twice what he was getting by his law practice and more congenial; besides it gave him the longed-for chance to get away from Great Barrington. But life as a "literary adventurer," as he called himself, was far from a bed of roses. Bryant worked like a galley-slave, and though he was the principal contributor of the *Review,* both in prose and verse, the paper drooped and well-nigh died. To enliven it, it was joined with the *Literary Gazette,* and Bryant accepted a quarter ownership and $500 per year salary. But things were no better. His confidence in the power of his pen became shaken, and he obtained a license to practice law in the courts of New York, thinking that he might again be obliged

> to drudge for the dregs of men,
> And scrawl strange words with a barbarous pen,
> And mingle among the jostling crowd
> Where the sons of strife are subtle and loud.

Bryant's poetry at this time showed the depressing influences about him, but never do we find anything but a trust in Divine Providence that all would come right in the end. Hear what he says in

THE JOURNEY OF LIFE

> Beneath the waning moon I walk at night,
> And muse on human life—for all around
> Are dim uncertain shapes that cheat the sight,
> And pitfalls lurk in shade along the ground,

And broken gleams of brightness, here and there,
Glance through, and leave unwarmed the deathless air.

The trampled earth returns a sound of fear—
    And hollow sound, as if I walked on tombs;
And lights, that tell of cheerful homes, appear,
    Far off, and die like hope amid the glooms.
A mournful wind across the landscape flies,
And the wide atmosphere is full of sighs.

And I with faltering footsteps journey on,
    Watching the stars that roll the hours away,
Till the faint light that guides me now is gone,
    And, like another life, the glorious day
Shall open o'er me from the empyreal height,
With warmth, and certainty, and boundless light.

Just as everything seemed darkest Bryant was offered a position as assistant editor of the *New York Evening Post*. This was an old well-known paper on a good paying foundation, and for the first time in his life Bryant found himself on his feet in a position to his liking. In three years the editor-in-chief died, and Bryant was chosen to fill his place. He already owned some shares in the plant, so he borrowed enough money to purchase a half interest. But Bryant's bad luck followed him; hard times came on and the *Post* well-nigh sank into the ground. Bryant became discouraged, and would have got out of the business and gone West, but no one would buy his interest and so he stuck to it, "to protect the interests of his creditors," he said. Finally diligence and unceasing toil had their reward. The paper grew and prospered and under Bryant's careful management became a beacon light. At his death his half interest was worth close to a million dollars.

Bryant always lived in the most careful and exact manner. Several of his family had died of consumption, and he had no mind to fall a prey to the disease if he could help it. He had no use for tobacco, except to quarrel with its use, as he said; never drank tea or coffee; and lived moderately, chiefly upon a vegetable and fruit diet.

In 1843 Bryant bought a beautiful country home on Long Island near the little village of Roslyn. The estate was called "Cedarmere," and was just such a nook as a poet might choose. The house was an old-fashioned mansion of many rooms, surrounded by shrubberies and grand trees, and a beautiful sloping lawn led down to a pretty little lake. Here with his wife and two daughters, Julia and Frances, he lived through the summer months the quiet happy life of a country gentleman and poet. His cares were left behind him in town and he gave himself up "to keeping his friendship in repair and to nursing the graces of garden and farm."

Mrs. Bryant was an invalid during the last few years of her life, and her husband made her comfort his especial care. She died July 27, 1866. Modest in her ways, she had lived wholly for her home. "Her husband's welfare, his happiness, and his fame were the chief objects of her ambition." Bryant wrote to his friend Dana, "I lived with my wife forty-five years, and now that great blessing of my life is withdrawn, and I am like one cast out of Paradise and wandering in a strange world."

William Cullen Bryant lived to a ripe old age, hale and hearty to the last, his death being caused by an over-exposure to the hot sun. He had been invited to give an address at the unveiling of the statue to Mazzini, the Italian patriot, in Central Park, and accepted most willingly, for he was an accomplished orator. His discourse was one of the best and most entertaining he ever made. But he stood too long in the sunlight, and on entering a friend's house after the exercises fell senseless in the doorway; his body lingered for two weeks, but he never regained consciousness. He died June 12, 1878.

Though a whole nation would proudly have honored his remains with a public funeral, the services were as private and simple as possible, according to his well-known wishes. He was laid to rest in the cemetery at Roslyn beside his beloved wife, whom he had mourned for twelve years.

Ralph Waldo Emerson

W HEN Frederika Bremer visited Boston, and Emerson called upon her, she wrote, "He came with a sunbeam on his countenance. He is a born gentleman." George William Curtis said, "At Emerson's house it is always morning."

How could it have been otherwise with a man who loved humanity; whose whole life was spent in making the world happier and better; whose every sentence was full of hope and sweetness and courage, who wrote, "To help the young soul, add energy, inspire hope, and blow the coals into a useful flame; to redeem defeat by new thought, by firm action, that is not easy; that is the work of divine men." And he was one of the noble men whose work in life it was to do this.

"Don't hang a dismal picture on the wall," he said, "and do not daub with sables and glooms in your conversation. Don't be a cynic and disconsolate preacher. Don't bewail and bemoan. Don't waste yourself in rejection, nor bark against the bad, but chant the beauty of the good. Never worry people with your contritions, nor with dismal views of politics or society. Never name sickness. . . . Set down nothing that will not help somebody." "Help somebody!" Such was the key-note of his life and his teaching.

"He who digs a well, constructs a stone fountain, plants a grove of trees by the roadside, plants an orchard, builds a dura-ble house, reclaims a swamp, or so much as puts a stone seat by the wayside, makes the land so far lovely and desirable, makes a fortune which he cannot carry away with him, but which is useful to his country long afterwards. . . . A man is a man only as he makes life and nature happier to us."

He preached a gospel of cheerfulness. "Good-nature is stronger than tomahawks," he said. . . . "How often it seems the chief good to be born with a cheerful temper, and well ad-justed to the tone of the human race. . . . Write it on your heart that every day is the best day in the year. . . . The scholar must be a bringer of hope."

How often he said to the young, "They can conquer who believe they can. . . . He has not learned the lesson of life who does not every day surmount a fear. . . . Hitch your wagon to a star. . . . Trust thyself: every heart vibrates to that iron string. . . . The man that stands by himself the universe will stand by him also. . . . Nature suffers nothing to remain in her kingdoms which cannot help itself. . . . The basis of good manners is self-reliance. . . . Self-trust is the first secret of success, the belief that, if you are here, the au-thorities of the universe put you here, and for cause, or with some task strictly appointed you in your constitution. . . . Welcome evermore to gods and men is the self-helping man. For him all doors are flung wide, him all tongues greet, all honors crown, all eyes follow with desire. Our love goes out to him, and embraces him because he did not need it."

I once heard Edward Everett Hale say, "You can never lead unless you lift," and Emerson always lifted. "When a man lives with God, his voice shall be sweet as the murmur of the brook and the rustle of the corn. . . . Do not rely on heavenly favor, or on compassion to folly, or on prudence, on common sense, the old usage and main chance of men: nothing can keep you,—not fate, nor health, nor admirable intellect; none can keep you, but rectitude only, rectitude for ever and ever! . . . Civilization depends on morality. . . . I am of the opinion of the poet Wordsworth, 'that there is no real happiness in this life, but in intellect and virtue.' I am of the opinion of Pliny, 'that, whilst we are musing on these things, we are adding to the length of our lives.' . . . I much prefer that my life should be of a lower strain so it be genuine and equal, than that it should be glittering and unsteady. I wish it to be sound and sweet."

Emerson wrote not for his time alone, but for all time. The world needs encouragement, and he encouraged; it needs ideals, and he gave ideals, beautified by his own beautiful spirit, for he said, "With the great ones thoughts and manners easily become great. . . . The earth waits for exalted manhood. What this country longs for is personalities, grand persons, to counteract its materialities."

And what of the history of this brother of the race? Did he have trials and sorrows like other mortals? Was character perfected, as it usually is, in a furnace?

Ralph Waldo Emerson, born in Boston, May 25, 1803, was descended from eight generations of ministers, true, sturdy men, who filled their places in the world nobly. His father, Rev. William Emerson, born in the Old Manse at Concord, Mass., immortalized by Hawthorne, was the pastor of the First Church in Boston; the mother, Ruth Haskins, a woman "whose mind and character were of a superior order, and they set their stamp upon manners of peculiar softness, natural grace, and quiet dignity." One of her sons said that when she came from her room in the morning it seemed to him as if she always came from communion with God, so sincere was her nature and so even her temper.

Ralph Waldo was the second of five sons, an amiable and obedient boy to his mother, who was left a widow when he was eight years old. So sensitive was he that once when reproved by his aunt for spending six cents in taking a novel from the circulating library, because his mother's means were so limited, he carried back the book unread, and for many years could not be prevailed upon to read it.

In the Boston Latin School he early showed poetical ability, translating at eleven a portion from the fifth Eclogue of Virgil into smooth verse, to please a lady. His aunt, Mary Moody Emerson, to whom he was much attached, was a great reader of Plato, Aristotle, Plotinus, Milton, Locke, Coleridge, and Byron. He said, in later years, that she had done more for him than Greece and Rome.

Sarah Bradford, his intimate friend, "the most learned woman ever seen in New England," asked Waldo to correspond with her in Latin and Greek, saying, "Tell me what most interests you in Rollin, and write me with what stories in Virgil you are delighted." Such friends were a stimulus to his mind.

He was extremely fond of history as well as Greek, but said later, "The regular course of studies, the years of academical and professional education, have not yielded me better facts than some idle books under the bench at the Latin School. What we do not call education is more precious than that which we do call so."

At fourteen, Waldo entered Harvard College, a slender, delicate youth, becoming "president's freshman," running on errands for him. Mrs. Emerson removed to Cambridge, taking some students into her home to board, while her son William opened a school in her house, and was assisted in teaching by Waldo. Evidently, there was little time for sports had the boy been so inclined.

Waldo had little love for or success in mathematics, and not much more in philosophy. He read carefully the old English poets, especially Shakespeare. Montaigne's essays he found delightful. He said in his later lecture years on Montaigne: "It seemed to me as if I had myself written the book in some former life, so sincerely it spoke to my thought and experience."

Edward Everett was his Greek professor, for whom he had the greatest admiration, following him from Sabbath to Sabbath as he preached in the different Boston churches, that he might not miss his eloquent sermons.

While in college, young Emerson wrote two poems as exercises, one to be given at a public exhibition. Taking it to one of his professors, Edward Channing, the only criticism was, "You had better write another poem." "What a useless remark was that," said Emerson, later; "he might at least have pointed out to me some things in my verses that were better than others, for all could not have been equally bad."

In his junior year he took the Bowdoin prize for a composition on the character of Socrates, and was Class Day Poet; though, as the honor was declined by seven others before he was asked, he was evidently not considered greatly superior to his fellows.

His college course ended, he went to Boston to assist his brother, who had opened a school for young ladies. It was not because teaching was to his taste, but he wanted to help his younger brothers through college.

At twenty he began to study for the ministry. Perhaps he was led to do this somewhat from the fact that his older brother had intended to become a preacher, but his doubts as

to matters of belief induced him to take up the law. Waldo
still taught in various schools, winning the love of his pupils.
His usual mode of punishment when the boys did wrong was,
says Dr. Holmes, a sorrowful look, with the words, "Oh, sad!"
But this brought the desired repentance and reformation, because the students could not bear to pain him.

All this time he was frail in body, so that when he was
ready for preaching, at twenty-three, he was obliged to go to
Florida and South Carolina for the winter. His eyes also troubled him so that he could not take notes in the lecture-room.
With poverty and poor health, the way did not look very
bright, and yet the young man kept his cheerful face and nature.

On his return, he was called to the Second Church in Boston, as the assistant of Rev. Henry Ware; but soon Mr. Ware
resigned, and all the labor came on Mr. Emerson. His sermons
were clear and eloquent. He was liked not only for these, but
because he took an active part in public work, being a member of the School Board and the chaplain of the State Senate.

The year of his ordination, when he was twenty-six, he married Ellen Louisa Tucker, and life seemed full of promise. To
her he had written that lovely poem *Ellen, at the South*.

But she did not stay with him long, for in three years consumption had taken her away and another chasm lay athwart
his life for him to bridge with hope and faith.

There were other troubles close at hand. Because his views
had changed with regard to church ordinances, especially the
administration of the Lord's Supper, he decided to resign his
pastorate. Many hearts were touched when the young thinker,
standing alone in his sorrow, gave up his prospects of honor
and success in the ministry, because he could not preach what
he did not believe. With never a harsh word for any in the
tumult of discussion that followed this step, he kept the even

tenor of his way, but his health broke under it, and in the following spring he sailed for Europe.

He first visited Sicily and Italy, then France and England. He modestly says in his *English Traits:* "My narrow and desultory reading had inspired the wish to see the faces of three or four writers,—Coleridge, Wordsworth, Landor, De Quincey, and the latest and strongest contributor to the critical journals, Carlyle. If Goethe had been still living, I might have wandered into Germany also."

In Florence he met Horatio Greenough, the artist, and afterward Landor, Coleridge, and Wordsworth. Best of all for both, he met Thomas Carlyle. "He was," says Emerson, "tall and gaunt, with a cliff-like brow, self-possessed, and holding his extraordinary powers of conversation in easy command. . . . We talked of books. Plato he does not read, and he disparaged Socrates. Gibbon he called the splendid bridge from the old world to the new. His own reading had been multifarious."

The friendship which developed helped to make each known more widely in the country of the other.

On his return from Europe, he looked about him to see where he should make his home. He chose the Concord of his ancestors, and thither he went, to the Old Manse, where lived his grandfather, Dr. Ripley. "I am a poet by nature," he said, "and therefore must live in the country." He was like the city boy whom he describes as going for the first time into the woods in October: "He is the king he dreamed he was; he walks through tents of gold, through bowers of crimson, porphyry, and topaz, pavilion on pavilion, garlanded with vines, flowers, and sunbeams, with incense and music."

What now should be his lifework? He loved study, but he must earn his living. He would try the lecture platform, and to that end he chose two subjects, *Water,* and *The Relation of Man to the Globe.* After this he gave three lectures upon his European experiences.

These were followed by a course in Boston, upon Luther, Milton, Burke, Michelangelo, and George Fox. These were liked, and won for him many friends. Then came an address before the American Institute of Instruction, on *The Means of Inspiring a Taste for English Literature,* and a historical address in Concord.

At the Old Manse, when he was thirty-three, he wrote his first book, *Nature,* of less than one hundred pages, of which only five hundred copies were sold in twelve years. Evidently, authorship would not buy bread, with such sales.

Three years and a half after the death of his first wife, he married Lydia Jackson, of Plymouth, Mass., a cultivated and sensible woman, and, fortunately, a woman with moderate means. A roomy, cheery home was purchased, with great horse chestnut trees in front, and garden and brook in the rear, and thither the two went to begin a life of peace and happiness.

He gave this year, 1835, a course of ten lectures in Boston on English literature, including Chaucer, Bacon, Shakespeare, Byron, Scott, Coleridge, and others; the next year, twelve on the Philosophy of History; the next, ten on Human Culture. Besides this, he was preaching twice each Sunday at East Lexington.

On April 19, 1836, at the completion of the Battle Monument, his immortal Concord Hymn was sung, to the tune of Old Hundred:

> By the rude bridge that arched the flood
>   Their flag to April's breeze unfurled,
> Here once the embattled farmers stood,
>   And fired the shot heard round the world.
>
> The foe long since in silence slept;
>   Alike the conqueror silent sleeps;

And Time the ruined bridge has swept
  Down the dark stream which seaward creeps

On this green bank, by this soft stream,
  We set to-day a votive stone;
That memory may their deed redeem,
  When, like our sires, our sons are gone.

Spirit, that made those heroes dare
  To die, and leave their children free,
Bid Time and Nature gently spare
  The shaft we raise to them and thee.

In the midst of this happiness and work, death had come twice into the Emerson circle, first taking a brilliant brother, Edward, who, studying law with Daniel Webster, broke down in health, and died in Puerto Rico; and then Charles, a young lawyer.

To Carlyle, Emerson wrote, "I have lost out of this world my brother Charles, the friend and companion of many years, the inmate of my house, a man of beautiful genius, born to speak well, and whose conversation for these last years has treated every grave question of humanity, and has been my daily bread. . . . He was to have been married in this month; and at the time of his sickness and sudden death I was adding apartments to my house for his permanent accommodation. At twenty-seven years the best life is only preparation."

And life as well as death had come into the Emerson home, in the birth of their little son Waldo. Emerson wrote to Moncure D. Conway, "Life is all preface until we have children; then it is deep and solid." At five months old the baby was "a loving wonder, that made the universe look friendlier," and when a little older, Emerson wrote Carlyle that his boy was a "piece of love and sunshine, well worth my watching from morning to night."

But four years later he had to write to Carlyle, "A few weeks ago I accounted myself a very rich man, and now the poorest of all. What would it avail to tell you anecdotes of a sweet and wonderful boy, such as we solace and sadden ourselves with at home, every morning and evening. From a perfect health, and as happy a life and as happy influences as ever child enjoyed, he was hurried out of my arms in three short days, by scarlatina. How often I have pleased myself that one day I should send to you this Morning Star of mine, and stay at home so gladly behind such a representative."

These were very busy and earnest years for Emerson. August 31, 1837, he spoke before the Phi Beta Kappa Society of Cambridge on *The American Scholar*. In that famous address he warned a generation of scholars as cowed by fear as our own that "the spirit of the American free man is already suspected to be timid, imitative, tame." Speaking at Harvard University, an institution that was sometimes attacked by American opponents of freedom because it dares to follow Emerson, the American philosopher expounded an idea as important today as it was in 1837. "Free should the scholar be," he says, "—free and brave. Free even to the definition of freedom. . . . Brave; for fear is a thing which a scholar by his very function puts behind him. Fear always springs from ignorance." And Emerson advised his audience to "henceforth defy it and pass on superior." In such accents did the great American teacher and scholar speak.

For a little time he edited the *Dial*, a magazine devoted to literature, philosophy, and religion. Then, at his own risk, he brought out *Sartor Resartus* from the essays in *Fraser's Magazine*, writing a preface for it, and realized seven hundred dollars for his friend Carlyle before the sketches had appeared in book form in England.

Emerson's first volume of essays was published in 1841,

when he was thirty-eight years old, and his second volume in 1844, upon such subjects as History, Self-Reliance, Intellect, Love, etc. The people could read and understand his terse sentences, which became way-marks in thought for a lifetime: "Though we travel the world over to find the beautiful, we must carry it with us or we find it not."

"Love and you shall be loved . . . all mankind loves a lover."

"The only way to have a friend is to be one."

"Nothing great was ever achieved without enthusiasm."

"The secret of success in society is a certain heartiness and sympathy. . . . Life is not so short but that there is always time enough for courtesy. . . . Self-command is the main elegance. 'Keep cool, and you command everybody,' said St. Just."

"Give me health and a day, and I will make the pomp of emperors ridiculous."

"No man can be a master in conversation who has not learned much from women; their presence and inspiration are essential to its success."

In 1847, Emerson sailed again for Europe, to give a series of lectures at the request of several prominent persons.

He lectured on Plato, Swedenborg, Shakespeare, Goethe, and others, to crowded audiences. In 1850 these lectures were published in a volume called *Representative Men,* which was well received.

He and his wife had three more children: Edith, now married; Ellen, who cheered his declining years; and Edward, a physician in Concord.

Emerson was a student of books, and therefore spent necessarily much of his time in solitude. He said, "The conditions of literary success are almost destructive of the best social power, as they do not leave that frolic liberty which only can encounter a companion on the best terms. . . . A self-denial, no less austere than the saint's, is demanded of the scholar. . . . He must embrace solitude as a bride. . . . Solitude, the safeguard of mediocrity, is to genius the stern friend, the cold, obscure shelter where moult the wings which will bear it farther than sun and stars. . . . The scholar must be a university of languages."

And yet, while he had little time for social life, he made time to discuss all the great questions in which America's future was concerned. He always had a voice in the anti-slavery movement, and early advocated buying the slaves—a plan which would have been the saving of many lives and fortunes.

He believed in suffrage for woman, and said, "It is very cheap wit that finds it so droll that a woman should vote."

In war times he spoke in Washington, and Lincoln came with his cabinet to see and listen to the great thinker. When, January 1, 1863, the Emancipation Proclamation was carried into effect, Emerson read, in his native city, his famous *Boston Hymn.*

Two years later he spoke on Lincoln's death terse, tender, golden words, which will be remembered as long as Abraham Lincoln is remembered, and that will be through eternity.

Already his *Conduct of Life* had been published, and twenty-five hundred copies were sold in two days. His words, "Make yourself necessary to the world and mankind will give you bread," had proved true.

When he was sixty-three, Harvard College conferred upon him the degree of Doctor of Laws, and made him one of her Governing Board. During three successive years he delivered before his Alma Mater courses of lectures on the *Natural History of the Intellect,* and spoke in other places. He used to say of his lecturing East and West that it was "a base necessity," but it was a blessing to the country, for it brought tens of thousands into personal contact with him.

In 1870 he brought out *Society and Solitude.*

The next year he visited California; and the next, Egypt and England. During his absence, his house, which had been nearly consumed by fire, was rebuilt by generous friends, at a cost of eleven thousand dollars; and upon his returning, May, 1873, a large procession met him with music, and escorted him, under triumphal arches, to his renovated home.

When he was seventy-one, he published *Parnassus,* a collection of favorite poems. In 1874, he received the nomination of Lord Rector of Glasgow University, and had five hundred votes, against seven hundred for Disraeli; an amazing number to be received by an American.

As late as 1880, when he was seventy-seven, he delivered his one-hundredth lecture before the Concord Lyceum, on *New England Life and Letters;* but his memory was failing, and only as his faithful daughter Ellen was near and aided him could the tired mind do its work.

Letters and Social Aims was now published. Societies asked in vain for more lectures; his day was drawing to its close.

I shall never forget a visit made to him a little before this time. The mind had lost something of the power I used to feel when I heard him lecture, but the voice had the same sweetness, the deep blue eyes were as blue as ever, and the ineffable smile one could never forget. As we talked of education for a boy, my own beloved son in mind, he giving advice, he said, modestly, "After all, I do not feel competent to judge." Who not, if not he, who had stood before the students of nearly every college, and knew their aims and methods by heart? He showed me a picture of Carlyle, and spoke of their abiding friendship.

The library was a place of special interest. Of course, one

found there his favorite books—Homer, Plato, Plutarch, of whom he had said, "He cannot be spared from the smallest library; first, because he is so readable, which is much; then, that he is medicinal and invigorating"; Dante, Shakespeare, Milton, Bacon, Montaigne, Scott, Goethe, and others, a generous number, on high, plain shelves. His habits of work were simple: work in the morning; walk and thought in the afternoon, jotting down in his little notebooks, which he always carried with him, any thought or quotation which pleased him. He once wrote Carlyle: "I jot evermore in my endless journal a line on every knowable in nature; but the arrangement loiters long, and I get a brick-kiln instead of a house."

His mind failed more and more. At Longfellow's funeral, Mr. Conway says Emerson remarked, after looking in the coffin, "That gentleman was a sweet, beautiful soul, but I have entirely forgotten his name."

A little later, he took a severe cold, and the end came shortly.

He passed away quietly, April 27, 1882, lacking only a few days of eighty years of age.

His grave was made beneath a tall pine tree, not far from the graves of Hawthorne and Thoreau, and completely lined with hemlock boughs.

Back of the noble writing was a noble life; beautiful in domestic relations, magnanimous to those who opposed him, strong under most trying circumstances, unselfish. Beyond almost all literary men on record, his life has been worthy of his words.

Nathaniel Hawthorne

WHEN Washington Irving had finished reading *The Scarlet Letter,* he exclaimed, "Masterly! Masterly!" Oliver Wendell Holmes wrote the author, "I think we have no romancer but yourself, nor have had any for this long time. . . . There is rich blood in Hester, and the flavor of the sweet fern and the bayberry tree are not truer to the soil than the native sweetness of our little Phœbe! The Yankee mind has, for the most part, budded and flowered in pots of English earth, but you have fairly raised yours as a seedling in the natural soil. My criticism has to stop here; the moment a fresh mind takes in the elements of the common life about us, and transfigures them, I am contented to enjoy and admire, and let others analyze. Otherwise I should be tempted to display my appreciating sagacity in pointing out a hundred touches, transcriptions of nature, of character, of sentiment, true as the daguerreotype, free as crayon sketching, which arrested me even in the midst of the palpitating story."

And yet, with all this praise, almost no other American author ever wrote under such persistent and continuous discouragement. But he was superior to circumstances, and won the the admiration and affection of posterity.

The only son of a sea captain, one of a family of true-hearted New England Puritans, Nathaniel Hawthorne came into the world at Salem, Mass., July 4, 1804. The father died when his boy was but four years old, leaving a young wife, who, crushed by this early sorrow, shut herself out from society, and lived for forty years, till her death, a lonely and secluded life.

Mrs. Hawthorne, with her three children, Elizabeth, Nathaniel, and Maria Louisa, went to the home of her father, after her husband's death, and while there, her brother, Robert Manning, decided to educate her attractive boy. He was a lover of books, reading *Pilgrim's Progress* when he was six years old, and as soon as he could passably understand them, Shakespeare, Milton, Pope, and Thomson. The *Castle of Indolence* was his especial delight.

When he was nine, he was struck on the foot by a ball, and, being lame for some time, he would lie on the floor and read from morning till night. With the first money he ever earned, he purchased Spenser's *Faerie Queene,* and was entirely happy when absorbed in its pages.

And yet he liked fun, was especially fond of animals, and had a passion for the sea. He used to say, "I should like to sail on and on forever, and never touch the shore again."

At fourteen, his family moved to Sebago Lake, Maine, where, he says, "I lived like a bird of the air, so perfect was the freedom I enjoyed. . . . Ah, how well I recall the summer days; also when, with my gun, I roamed at will through the woods of Maine! . . . Everything is beautiful in youth, for all things are allowed to it then. . . . Though it was there I first got my cursed habits of solitude."

Here he continued to read everything he could find: the

Waverley Novels, Rousseau, and the *Newgate Calendar,* which was, perhaps, suggestive to him, in later years, in his pictures of crime.

He used to invent long stories, wild and fanciful, and tell where he was going when he grew up, and of the wonderful adventures he was to meet with, always ending with, "And I'm never coming back again," in quite a solemn tone. He was haunted with the idea that he should die before he reached the age of twenty-five, as he was in frail health, but kind care saved him for manhood.

At sixteen, the natural bias showed itself in the starting of a weekly paper, called *The Spectator,* to which he seems to have been the only contributor, and well-nigh the only subscriber, for, after six issues, he said, "We are sorry to be under the necessity of informing our readers that no deaths of any importance have taken place, except that of the publisher of this paper, who died of starvation, owing to the slenderness of his patronage."

A year later he entered Bowdoin College, along with Longfellow and Franklin Pierce. "He was at this time," says Julian Hawthorne, his son, "the handsomest young man of his day in that part of the world." Such is the report of those who knew him; and there is a miniature of him, taken some years later, which bears out this report. He was five feet ten and a half inches in height, broad-shouldered, but of a light, athletic build, not weighing more than one hundred and fifty pounds. His limbs were beautifully formed, and the moulding of his neck and throat was as fine as anything in antique sculpture. His hair, which had a long, curving wave in it, approached blackness in color; his head was large and grandly developed; his eyebrows were dark and heavy, with a superb arch and space beneath; his nose was straight, but the contour of his chin was Roman; his eyes were large, dark blue, brilliant, and full of varied expression. Bayard Taylor used to say that they were the only eyes he had ever known flash fire. Charles Reade declared that he had never before seen such eyes as Hawthorne's in a human head.

In college young Hawthorne enjoyed especially his English studies, and excelled in Latin composition. He had dreams of authorship. He wrote to his mother, "I do not want to be a doctor and live by men's diseases; nor a minister, to live by their sins; nor a lawyer, and live by their quarrels. So I don't see that there is anything left for me but to be an author. How would you like some day to see a whole shelf full of books written by your son, with 'Hawthorne's Works' printed on their backs?"

During these years, he wrote several poems and many sketches. George Parsons Lathrop, in his very interesting *Study of Hawthorne,* tells how he gathered some of these sketches together with the title, *Seven Tales of my Native Land,* and offered them first to one publisher and then to another, always with the same disheartening refusal. Finally a young printer of Salem promised to publish the book, but kept the manuscript so long that Hawthorne insisted upon its return, and at once burned it.

About this time he had written and published anonymously, at his own expense (one hundred dollars), a small novel entitled *Fanshawe.* It had little sale, and he never openly acknowledged it as his work, but a copy of it today, in good condition, would bring a price of several hundreds of dollars.

College days over, the outlook for literary pursuits was not inviting. His classmate, Pierce, went into the law, and Longfellow into a professorship, but Hawthorne went to his quiet home in Salem, to dream over his brilliant stories, and find no audience, save his own retiring family. For nearly twelve years he lived this secluded life, rarely going upon the Salem streets by daylight, and writing for the very few journals in which he could find an opening. No wonder he wrote, long afterwards, "I sat down by the wayside of life like a man under enchantment, and a shrubbery sprang up around me, and the bushes grew to be saplings, and the saplings became trees until no exit appeared possible through the entangling depths of my obscurity. . . ."

All these years he was reading intently. Lives of Mohammed, Pitt, Goldsmith, Coleridge, Shelley, Keats; books of travel, natural history, poetry, fiction, especially Scott and De Quincey, and encyclopædias; four hundred books in seven years, besides piles of magazines. Nothing seemed to escape his absorbent mind. Sir Philip Sidney's *Arcadia* he had read and re-read, till it was nearly worn out.

Finally he was asked to edit the *American Magazine of Useful Knowledge,* published in Boston, for which he received little fame and less pay, and did an enormous amount of hard work.

In 1837, Hawthorne, having collected a few of his stories, published them under the title, *Twice-Told Tales*. In the pathetic preface he said, "The author of *Twice-Told Tales* has a claim to one distinction, which, as none of his literary brethren will care about disputing it with him, he need not be afraid to mention. He was for a good many years the obscurest man of letters in America."

If authorship, with its hard, vexatious work, had not brought the means of support, one joy, at least, had come to him. He had said, "Even a young man's bliss has not been mine. With a thousand vagrant fantasies, I have never truly loved, and perhaps shall be doomed to loneliness throughout the eternal future, because, here on earth, my soul has never married itself to the soul of woman."

But he was not doomed to eternal loneliness. In Salem lived Doctor Peabody, with his wife and three gifted daughters; Elizabeth, the well-known author and teacher; Mary, who married Horace Mann; and Sophia. One evening,—an unusual occurrence,—the Hawthornes called upon the Peabody family. Elizabeth ran upstairs to the chamber of Sophia, who was an invalid, saying, "O Sophia, you must get up and dress and come down! The Hawthornes are here, and you never saw anything so splendid as he is,—he is handsomer than Lord Byron!"

She laughed and refused to go down, saying that, since he had called once, he would call again. He did call again, and Sophia came down in her simple white wrapper to see him. Elizabeth noticed that every time Sophia spoke, Hawthorne looked at her intently, "with the same piercing, indrawing gaze." "I was struck with it," she said, "and thought, 'What if he should fall in love with her!' and the thought troubled me; for she had often told me that nothing would ever tempt her to marry and inflict on a husband the care of an invalid."

From that hour, they were all the world to each other. They breasted poverty, they basked in the full glory of fame and honor, and love grew brighter and brighter, till death made it unending. Sophia Peabody changed the loneliness of the great-hearted student into peace and perfect satisfaction. She was his inspiration, his guide and continual blessing.

In 1839, through the influence of Bancroft, the historian, who was collector at Boston, Hawthorne obtained the position of weigher and gauger in the Boston Custom House. The work was hard, as he says in his *American Note-Books,* "My life is only a burden in the same way that it is to every toilsome man; and mine is a healthy weariness, such as needs only a night's sleep to remove it. But from henceforth forever I shall be entitled to call the sons of toil my brethren, and shall know how to sympathize with them, seeing that I, likewise, have risen at dawn and borne the fervor of the midday sun, nor turned my heavy footsteps homeward till eventide."

For two years he worked there, and for a third at Brook Farm, that dream of pure-hearted humanitarians, always cheered by the hope of wedding Sophia Peabody. He wrote to her, "I invite your spirit to be with me,—at any hour, and as many hours as you please,—but especially at the twilight hour, before I light my lamp. . . . If you cannot grow plump and rosy and tough and vigorous without being changed into another nature, then I do think, for this short life, you had better remain just what you are. Yes; but you will be the same to me, because we have met in Eternity, and there our intimacy was formed. I never till now had a friend who could give me repose; all have disturbed me, and, whether for pleasure or pain, it was still disturbance. But peace overflows from your heart into mine. . . . It is very singular that while I love you so dearly, and while I am conscious of the deep union of our spirits, still I have an awe of you that I never felt for anybody else. . . . I suppose I should have pretty much the same feeling if an angel were to come from Heaven and be my dearest friend,—only the angel could not have the tenderest of human natures, too, the sense of which is mingled with this sentiment."

And Sophia answered, "I am full of the glory of the day. God bless you this night of the old year. It has proved the year of our nativity. Has not the old year passed away from us?—are not all things new?"

Sophia eventually recovered her health, and they were married on July 9, 1842. Hawthorne was now thirty-eight, his bride thirty-two. They began their wedded life at the Old Manse in Concord, where Emerson had written his *Nature,* and where Hawthorne was to write his delightful *Mosses.* The wife, cheerful, hopeful, and, what was best of all, believing that her husband had brilliant talents, made his home a delight. She read Latin, Greek, and Hebrew, and was, as every woman must be who has lasting influence with her husband, his companion intellectually.

Six months after marriage, Sophia wrote her mother, "His will is strong, but not to govern others. He is so simple, so transparent, so just, so tender, so magnanimous, that my highest instinct could only correspond with his will."

As the months went by, the earnings did not always suffice for daily needs, and what money was due could not always be collected. Again the brave wife wrote to her mother, "But, somehow or other, I do not care much, because we are so happy. . . . The darker the shadow behind him, the more dazzling is his figure drawn to my sight. I must esteem myself happiest of women, whether I wear tow or velvet, or live in a log cabin or in a palace."

In these days of poverty, Hawthorne wrote in his *Note-Book*, "The chief event of the afternoon, and the happiest one of the day, is our walk. She must describe these walks; for when she and I have enjoyed anything together, I always deem my pen unworthy and inadequate to record it.

"My wife is, in the strictest sense, my sole companion, and I need no other; there is no vacancy in my mind any more than in my heart. In truth, I have spent so many years in total seclusion from all human society that it is no wonder if now I feel all my desires satisfied by this sole intercourse. But she has come to me from the midst of many friends and a large circle of acquaintance; yet she lives from day to day in this solitude, seeing nobody but myself and our Molly, while the snow of our avenue is untrodden for weeks by any footstep save mine; yet she is always cheerful. Thank God that I suffice for her boundless heart!"

After four years in Concord, where their first child, Una, was born, they returned to Salem, where Hawthorne had been appointed surveyor in the Custom House. This position he held for four years, till a change of President gave his place to another of different political views. The salary had been sufficient to support his wife and two children, their son Julian having been added to the household; but when this was withdrawn, the outlook was not hopeful.

Just at this time, James T. Fields, the publisher, who had heard that Hawthorne had been ill, came to Salem to see him, and thus describes the incident in his charming *Yesterdays with Authors:* "I found him alone in a chamber over the sitting-room of the dwelling; and, as the day was cold, he was hovering near a stove. We fell into talk about his future prospects, and he was, as I feared I should find him, in a very desponding mood. 'Now,' said I, 'is the time for you to publish, for I know, during these years in Salem, you must have got something ready for the press.'

" 'Nonsense,' said he, 'what heart had I to write anything, when my publishers have been so many years trying to sell a small edition of the *Twice-Told Tales.* Who would risk publishing a book for *me,* the most unpopular writer in America?'

" 'I would,' said I, 'and would start with an edition of two thousand copies of anything you write.' "

As Mr. Fields took his departure, Hawthorne put in his hands the germ of *The Scarlet Letter,* which the publisher read that night, and was delighted with it. At once the author began to amplify his work, and, when it was finished, read the conclusion to his wife, or, as he says, "tried to read it, for my voice swelled and heaved as if I were tossed up and down on an ocean as it subsides after a storm. It broke her heart, and sent her to bed with a grievous headache,—which I look upon as a triumphant success."

The book was published in 1850, and in ten days five thousand copies had been sold. England saw the new hand in literature, and gave it praise. At last, at forty-six, after all the burning of manuscripts, a fire had been kindled in human hearts that would never go out. Henceforward, instead of being the friend of Emerson and Longfellow and a chosen few, he was to be the admired of tens of thousands who would never be able to look upon his face.

What joy must have come into the heart that wrote previously, in his chamber, "Here I sat a long, long time, waiting patiently for the world to know me, and sometimes wondering why it did not know me sooner, or whether it would ever know me at all,—at least, till I were in my grave. And sometimes it seemed as if I were already in the grave, with only life enough to be chilled and benumbed. . . . And now I begin to understand why I was imprisoned so many years in this lonely chamber, and why I could never break through the viewless bolts and bars; for, if I had sooner made my escape into the world, I should have grown hard and rough, and been covered with earthy dust, and my heart might have become callous by rude encounters with the multitude. . . . But, living in solitude till the fulness of time was come, I still kept the dew of my youth and the freshness of my heart."

The next year, he moved to Lenox, where Rose, the third child, was born. There he wrote *The House of the Seven Gables* in five months, which, like *The Scarlet Letter*, became a favorite at once.

His next volume was the *Wonder-Book*, for children, containing the story of *Midas, Pandora's Box, Hercules in Quest of the Golden Apples*, and other classic tales.

The Blithedale Romance, founded upon the Brook Farm community, was published in 1852. This was about the time he bought Mr. Alcott's home in Concord, with twenty acres, and called it "The Wayside."

Life, with fame for her beloved husband, was full of blessing to Mrs. Hawthorne. She wrote, eight years after marriage: "I cannot possibly conceive of my happiness, but, in a blissful kind of confusion, live on."

Concord was a place of delightful rest for the tired man, who had written five books in three years, and had earned both fame and a fair competency. The world usually discovers its geniuses, sooner or later, but sometimes when they are beyond the hearing of earthly praise.

Here in Concord, where he could enjoy trees and sunshine, those essentials to a poetic nature, Hawthorne wrote his *Tanglewood Tales,* and a life of his classmate, Franklin Pierce, then a candidate for the Presidency. He said: "I tried to persuade Pierce that I could not perform it as well as many others; but he thought differently, and, of course, after a friendship of thirty years, it was impossible to refuse my best efforts in his behalf at the great pinch of his life."

It was Hawthorne's custom to walk several hours a day on a ridge back of the house; his "Mount of Vision," his wife called it, where he wore a narrow path, two or three hundred yards long. He planned his books in this quiet spot, and gained rest for closer work indoors.

After the election of Pierce, Mr. Hawthorne was appointed Consul to Liverpool, and sailed for England with his family March 26, 1853, when their long-wished-for opportunity of seeing the Old World was realized. There, of course, he was honored for his talents, and respected for his faithful discharge of official duties.

From Mr. Francis Bennoch, a cultured English gentleman, in London, one of Hawthorne's warmest friends, I learned much concerning the author's genuineness of heart and ten-

der, humane spirit. Here he met the Brownings, Florence
Nightingale, Coventry Patmore, and other prominent men
and women. Here he wrote his *English Note-Books,* which
thousands of us have read carefully and reverently as we have
lingered among the English Lakes or stood in the grand cathedrals.

After the Liverpool Consulship, the Hawthorne family
went to Italy, where, with a mind full of art and love, he wrote
The Marble Faun—his masterpiece, if we except *The Scarlet
Letter.* The Brownings had come to live in Florence, and they
made the Italian episode one beautiful holiday.

On their return to England, Hawthorne finished his *Romance at Redcar,* in Yorkshire, and it was published simul-
taneously in England and America, March, 1860. There was
some disappointment at the conclusion of the story; but admiration of the power and style of the book was universal.

In June of this year the family returned to America, to the
quiet "Wayside," at Concord. The Civil War had begun, and
Hawthorne's heart was too heavy for much literary work. He,
however, produced *Our Old Home* from his note-books, and
Septimius Felton.

The hand that held the pen was becoming weary. He grew
pale and thin, and in the spring and summer of 1863 went
southward for his health, with his friend and publisher, W. D.
Ticknor, who died suddenly, leaving Hawthorne greatly reduced by the shock and sorrow.

On his return Mrs. Hawthorne cared for him tenderly. She
wrote Mr. Fields: "I do nothing but sit with him, ready to
do or not to do, just as he wishes. He is my world, and all the
business of it. He has not smiled since he came home till today, and I made him laugh with Thackeray's humor in reading to him; but a smile looks strange on a face that once
shone like a thousand suns with smiles. The light, for the

time, has gone out of his eyes entirely. An infinite weariness films them quite."

Again he left home, in the middle of May, this time with his friend, ex-President Pierce. They reached Plymouth, New Hampshire, and stopped at the Pemigewasset House. Both friends retired early to their adjoining rooms. Several times Mr. Pierce came in to see if his friend slept well. After midnight he entered, and, not hearing him breathe, put his hand on Hawthorne's heart, and found that it had stopped beating.

The body was brought back to the bereaved wife and children, and buried in the little cemetery on the hilltop, near where Emerson now rests. His unfinished romance was laid upon his coffin. Rev. James Freeman Clarke, who had married them twenty-two years before, conducted the funeral services. As the wife left the open grave, on either side of the path stood Longfellow, Holmes, Whittier, Lowell, Emerson, Agassiz, Pierce, and others with uncovered heads, testifying their respect and sympathy.

The struggles and successes of authorship were over and Longfellow paid tribute for all America to her first great novelist.

Henry Wadsworth Longfellow

CHARLES KINGSLEY said, "I do not think I ever saw a finer human face."

I remember having much the same feeling when I saw for the first time the famous poet, in his home at Cambridge. His thick, fine hair was snowy white, his eyes blue and kindly, his voice melodious, and his whole bearing gentle.

The study where he sat was well filled with books, one case having his own manuscripts in substantial bindings; the table where he wrote was covered with letters; the quaint inkstand which he used once belonged to Coleridge, when he wrote the *Rime of the Ancient Mariner;* on the wall hung portraits of three noble friends, Emerson, Hawthorne, and Sumner. Out of the windows we looked upon the lilacs in blossom, the green meadows, and beyond, the Charles River.

The "fine human face" was but an index of the fine human heart; an index of a bright mind, pure character, and generous nature. Nobody was ever turned away from that home with a heavy heart. A young Pole came, wanting to lecture on the Italian Revolution. The great poet tried to dissuade him, knowing that it would lead to disappointment, but he "kept him to dinner and comforted him so that he departed in better spirits."

A schoolgirl, a stranger, wrote for an original poem! "I could not write it," said Mr. Longfellow, "but I tried to say *no* so softly that she would think it better than *yes.*"

In the height of his fame, when the great of Europe and America came to Craigie House,—Froude, Trollope, Kingsley, Dean Stanley, Dickens, Emperor Dom Pedro, Agassiz, Jenny Lind, and Mrs. Stowe (who, he said, "at one step has reached the top of the staircase up which the rest of us climb on our knees year after year")—he could take time to go to the Police Court to get the fines of a poor German woman remitted for stealing some apples.

So busy with work that he rose at five o'clock in the morning, he could take time to send off seventy-five autographs in one day, because somebody in this wide world would be made happier thereby.

A young and unknown poet asked for five minutes, and Longfellow, helpful toward all human things, gave him two hours, to hear his poems, and advise with him about his future. When he saw a shoe-dealer giving new shoes to a little beggar girl, he asked to share in the gift.

The second in a family of eight children, Henry W. Longfellow came into the old-fashioned Portland home February 27, 1807. The mother, a descendant of John Alden of the *Mayflower,* was the daughter of General Peleg Wadsworth, Adjutant-General of Massachusetts in the Revolutionary War; the father, Stephen Longfellow, a graduate from Harvard University, was an honored lawyer, noted for character no less than for scholarship.

From the mother must have come the boy's poetic nature. She was an ardent lover of sunshine, flowers, music, and poetry, always cheerful and the sharer of every secret joy or sorrow of her children.

The child Henry grew into boyhood affectionate, eager, and sensitive. He was "remarkably solicitous to do right," said his mother. "Injustice in any shape he could not brook," wrote his sister. Once when he had shot a robin, he came home with his eyes full of tears, so grieved that he never tried shooting again.

He was early fond of reading. "Every reader," he said years afterward, "has his first book; I mean to say, one book among all others which first fascinates his imagination, and at once excites and satisfies the desires of his mind. To me, this first book was the *Sketch-Book* of Washington Irving. . . . How many delightful books the same author has given us. . . . Yet still the charm of the *Sketch-Book* remains unbroken; the old fascination remains about it; and whenever I open its pages, I open also that mysterious door which leads back into the haunted chambers of youth." Of Cowper's poetry, Moore's *Lalla Rookh, Don Quixote,* and *Ossian,* the lad was very fond.

In the summer vacations he used to go to his grandfather Wadsworth's estate of seven thousand acres, just out of Portland, Maine, and listen with delight to the stirring tales of '76. The story of a fight with the Indians made a deep impression upon him, and at thirteen he wrote his first poem, *The Battle of Lovell's Pond.*

> Cold, cold is the north wind and rude is the blast
> That sweeps like a hurricane loudly and fast,
> As it moans through the tall waving pines lone and drear,
> Sighs a requiem sad o'er the warrior's bier.

> The war-whoop is still, and the savage's yell
> Has sunk into silence along the wild dell;
> The din of the battle, the tumult, is o'er,
> And the war-clarion's voice is now heard no more.

The warriors that fought for their country—and bled
Have sunk to their rest; the damp earth in their bed,
No stone tells the place where their ashes repose,
Nor points out the spot from the graves of their foes.

They died in their glory, surrounded by fame,
And Victory's loud trump their death did proclaim;
They are dead; but they live in each Patriot's breast,
And their names are engraven on honor's bright crest.

—HENRY

He cautiously slipped the manuscript into the letterbox, telling no one but his sister, and waited anxiously to see if the important production appeared in the columns of the *Portland Gazette*. Scarcely able to wait, he soothed his mind by going to the newspaper office, and walking in front of the building, shivering in a cold November morning, and fancying, as the types were set, that his poem was going into immortal print.

The next day it appeared, and Henry read and reread it, while each time it seemed more beautiful. In the evening, he went to the house of a friend, Judge Mellen, who said, "Did you see the piece of poetry in to-day's paper? Very stiff, remarkably stiff; moreover, it is all borrowed, every word of it."

The boy's heart sank within him, and he hurried home to sob himself to sleep. No wonder that he wrote, years later, in *Kavanagh:* "I feel a kind of reverence for the first books of young authors. There is so much aspiration in them, so much audacious hope and trembling fear, so much of the heart's history, that all errors and shortcomings are for a while lost sight of." . . . Long afterward he said, "The ill will of anybody hurts me. If a critic cannot speak well of a book, why speak of it at all? The best criticism of an unworthy book . . . is silence."

These were all precious years, leaving their impress for a great work in the future. *My Lost Youth* tells of these.

> Often I think of the beautiful town
>   That is seated by the sea;
> Often in thought go up and down
> The pleasant streets of that dear old town,
>   And my youth comes back to me.
>   And a verse of a Lapland song
>   Is haunting my memory still:
>   "A boy's will is the wind's will,
> And the thoughts of youth are long, long thoughts."
>
> I remember the gleams and glooms that dart
>   Across the school-boy's brain;
> The song and the silence in the heart,
> That in part are prophecies, and in part
>   Are longings wild and vain.
>   And the voice of that fitful song
>   Sings on, and is never still:
>   "A boy's will is the wind's will,
> And the thoughts of youth are long, long thoughts."

When Henry was fourteen, he entered Bowdoin College, where his father was one of the trustees. Here he was an earnest student, especially fond of Horace, but not skilled in mathematics. He had, says Professor Packard, "unblemished character as a pupil, and was a true gentleman in all his relations with the college and its teachers."

To his mother he wrote his ideas of Johnson, Gray, and other authors; and she in turn responded with her opinions. During his college course he wrote several poems, only five of which he cared to publish in book form afterward. One of these, the *Hymn of the Moravian Nuns of Bethlehem,* and *Burial of the Minnisink,* written before he was nineteen, were much liked. For most of these he was promised pay at the rate of two dollars a column, but received finally, instead of money, Chatterton's works, in three volumes, which gave great pleasure as they were the first earnings of his pen.

As the time drew near for him to leave college, he wrote his father, "I want to spend one year at Cambridge for the purpose of reading history and of becoming familiar with the best authors in polite literature. . . . The fact is, I most eagerly aspire after future eminence in literature; my whole soul burns most ardently for it, and every earthly thought centers in it. . . . Whatever I do study ought to be engaged in with all my soul,—for I *will be eminent* in something. . . . I have a most voracious appetite for knowledge. To its acquisition I will sacrifice everything."

His father wrote back: "A literary life, to one who has the means of support, must be very pleasant. . . . As you have not had the fortune (I will not say whether good or ill) to be born rich, you must adopt a profession which will afford you subsistence as well as reputation."

Young Longfellow graduated fourth in a class of thirty-eight, and reluctantly turned toward the law.

Fortunately, there was something more congenial in store for him. One of the trustees had been especially pleased with his translation of an ode from Horace, and proposed his name for the Professorship of Modern Languages, just created at Bowdoin, suggesting that he spend three years in study in Europe to make himself ready for the position. This was welcome news indeed.

At nineteen the young man started for the Old World, and after a thirty-day voyage in a sailing packet, ocean steamers being unknown, reached Paris. His first letter from his mother read, "May you hold fast your integrity, and retain that purity of heart which is so endearing to your friends. I feel as if you were going into a thousand perils." And a cheerful letter came back: "I feel as happy as possible; am in the best health in the world, and am delighted with Paris, where a person, if he pleases, can keep out of vice as well as elsewhere."

He lived economically and worked hard at his studies. He wrote to his father, "The truth is that the heavy responsibility which I have taken upon myself . . . and the fear that you will be displeased about my expenses are hanging with a terrible weight upon me."

The first autumn, in October, which to the end of his life was the most beautiful month of the year to him, he took a long journey on foot, and then spent eight months in Spain. Washington Irving was at Madrid, preparing his *Life of Columbus.* "He seemed to be always at work," said Longfellow. "One summer morning, passing his house at the early hour of six, I saw his study window already wide open. On my mentioning it to him afterwards, he said, 'Yes, I am always at my work as early as six.' "

He visited Italy for a year, enjoying the sculptures of Florence, the Bay of Naples, Rome, Venice ("the most wonderful city I ever beheld"), Vienna, and Prague, and then went to Germany. He wrote to his sisters, urging them to study the languages, saying that he was "completely enchanted" with them; that he spoke the French and Spanish as easily as English, read Portuguese without difficulty, and at the hotels was taken for an Italian from his excellent pronunciation of their language.

At Dresden, letters from Irving opened to him all literary and social advantages, and at Göttingen letters from Bancroft and Ticknor did the same. All this time the correspondence with his mother was an especial comfort. "For me," he wrote her, "a line from my mother is more efficacious than all the homilies preached in Lent, and I find more incitement to virtue in merely looking at your handwriting than in a whole volume of ethics and moral discourses. Indeed, there is no book in which I read with so much interest and profit as one of your letters."

At twenty-two he returned to America, and began his work at Bowdoin College with zest and hope. This year, 1829, he translated for his students a French grammar, and edited a collection of French proverbs and a small Spanish reader, for he said, "The young mind must be interested in order to be instructed."

Though not expected to do more than teach the languages, his interest in his work led him to prepare written lectures upon French, Spanish, and Italian literatures.

The new professor became deeply loved for his sympathy and aid. Besides, he was young, and has youth not a special charm of its own? His manner of dealing with students was very happy and efficacious as well. He was requested to admonish one of them, and the next day, meeting the person on the street, after an earnest talk about French literature, Longfellow said, "Ah! I was near forgetting. The Faculty voted last night that I should admonish you, and you will consider yourself admonished." At another time, when one of his pupils was audibly helped by another, he remarked, "Your recitation reminds me of the Spanish theater, where the prompter performs a more important part than the actor."

Two years later Longfellow married Mary Storer Potter, the second daughter of Judge Potter, of Portland. The marriage seemed to bring the young couple complete happiness.

His first book, a translation from the Spanish, of ninety pages, was published in 1833, two years after marriage, and *Outre-Mer* in 1834, sketches of travel. He wrote to a friend in Europe, "You see I am pushing on with vigor. There is nothing like writing when one is in the vein. The moment you stop, you grow cool; and then it is all over with you."

But Longfellow desired a broader sphere, and one soon opened through the interest in him of Mr. Ticknor, who was about to resign the Professorship of Modern Languages at Harvard University. It was offered to Longfellow, who, after five and a half years at Bowdoin, accepted, and decided to spend eighteen months in Europe in study before entering upon his duties.

Taking his wife with him, they spent some months in Stockholm, where he studied Swedish, then Danish and Finnish, and later, in Holland, the Dutch language and literature.

With all this happiness and prospective honor, a deep shadow was close at hand. Mrs. Longfellow died at Rotterdam, November 29, 1835, saying with her last breath, "I will be with you and watch over you."

That his grief was almost insupportable, we learn from *Hyperion,* published four years later. "The setting of a great hope is like the setting of the sun. The brightness of our life is gone. Shadows of evening fall around us, and the world seems but a dim reflection,—itself a broader shadow. We look forward into the coming lonely night. The soul withdraws into itself. Then stars arise, and the night is holy."

To his father he wrote, "Every day makes me more conscious of the loss I have suffered in Mary's death; and when I think how gentle and affectionate and good she was every moment of her life, even to the last, and that she will be no more with me in this world,—the sense of my bereavement is deep and unutterable."

Of her he wrote, three years later, his touching poem, *Footsteps of Angels.*

After his wife's death, Longfellow visited Heidelberg, Switzerland, and the Tyrol, returning to America in December, 1836, and entering upon his work at Harvard. He soon drew around him a circle of devoted friends, among them

Sumner, Prescott, Hawthorne, and Emerson. He began lecturing on the Languages of the South of Europe, Anglo-Saxon Literature, German Literature, and kindred topics.

He took pleasant rooms at Craigie House, a large, old-fashioned, yellow-and-white building, where General Washington and his wife lived when he assumed the command of the American army. Here poetry, of which he had written scarcely a verse for several years, seemed to take possession of his heart anew. One bright summer morning, July 26, 1836, on the blank portion of a note of invitation, he wrote *The Psalm of Life*. He said, "I kept it some time in manuscript, unwilling to show it to anyone—it being a voice from my inmost heart, at a time when I was rallying from depression."

The years were full of work, but Longfellow was often restless. In 1838 he wrote in his journal: "I do not like this sedentary life. I want action. I want travel. . . . After all, I pray a benediction on drudgery. It occupies my thoughts and takes the fever out of my blood, and keeps me from moping too much. But the time speeds away almost too fast."

The latter part of 1838 he wrote, "with peace in my heart and not without tears in my eyes," *The Reaper and the Flowers,* which was greatly liked. When it was read to the wife of his life-long friend, Professor Felton, she wept like a child. Longfellow said, "I want no more favorable criticism than this."

The next year the publication of *Hyperion* won hearty approval, though, unfortunately, the publisher failed, and half the edition of twelve hundred was seized by the creditors. "The name of the book indicates," said Longfellow, "that here is the life of one who in his feelings and purposes is a 'son of Heaven and Earth,' and who, though obscured by clouds, yet moves on high."

The following year, 1839, a small volume of poems, *Voices*

of the Night, was published, and in three weeks a thousand copies were sold. This year also, December 30, the *Ballad of the Schooner Hesperus* was written. There had been a terrible storm along the coast, and many vessels had gone to pieces on the rocks, the *Hesperus* among them. At midnight the idea came into Longfellow's mind to write the ballad, as he sat before his fire, having just written a notice of All-ston's poems for the press. He wrote it, and "went to bed, but could not sleep. New thoughts were running in my mind, and I got up to add them to the ballad. It was three by the clock," he wrote in his journal.

In 1840 he composed *The Skeleton in Armor,* as well as *The Spanish Student,* a drama in five acts, and in the following year he wrote *Excelsior,* the manuscript of which is now to be seen in the Harvard College Library.

One day, Mr. Longfellow's eye fell upon a piece of newspaper bearing the seal of the State of New York, a shield with a rising sun, and the motto in Latin, "Excelsior." At once he imagined the Alpine youth, and made him "a symbol of the aspiration and sacrifice of a nobly ideal soul." This poem and *Maidenhood* the poet thought "as good as anything he had written." They appeared in *Ballads, and Other Poems,* published in 1841.

Somewhat broken in health, in 1842 he went to Europe the third time, going to Bruges, where he "rose before five and climbed the high belfry."

At this time he wrote *Mezzo Cammin,* first published in Rev. Samuel Longfellow's beautiful and sympathetic life of his brother:

> Half of my life is gone, and I have let
>   The years slip from me and have not fulfilled
>   The aspiration of my youth, to build
>   Some tower of song with lofty parapet.

Not indolence, nor pleasure, nor the fret
  Of restless passions that would not be stilled,
  But sorrow, and a care that almost killed,
Kept me from what I may accomplish yet;
Though, half-way up the hill, I see the Past
  Lying beneath me with its sounds and sights,—
  A city in the twilight dim and vast,
With smoking roofs, soft bells, and gleaming lights,—
  And hear above me on the autumnal blast
  The cataract of Death far thundering from the heights.

On the voyage home, though in his berth much of the passage, he wrote several poems on Slavery, and published them in a pamphlet on his return. Of course some persons were sorry that he had touched so unpopular a subject; but a friend wrote him, "By those poems your name is fastened to an immortal truth."

For some years the poet's heart had been turning toward a lovely young woman, the daughter of Nathan Appleton, a prominent Boston merchant, whom he had met six years before in Switzerland; the Mary Ashburton of *Hyperion*.

She was then a beautiful girl of nineteen; now she was twenty-five, intellectual, and beautiful. Longfellow was married to Frances Elizabeth Appleton on July 13, 1843; he was thirty-six. The bride's father purchased Craigie House for their home, with several acres of land across the street, that they might keep an unobstructed view of the Charles River.

Their wedding journey was made to the wife's friends at Pittsfield, where stood the "old clock on the stairs" upon which the familiar poem was written. Passing through Springfield, they visited the Arsenal, and at the suggestion of the bride a peace poem was written, *The Arsenal at Springfield,* a favorite with the poet.

A short time before his marriage, he had strained his eyes

by using them in the twilight, and his wife acted as his aman-
uensis. This autumn he edited, with her help and that of
Professor Felton, *Poets and Poetry of Europe,* four hundred
pages in double column.

Then *Evangeline* was begun, the story being told to him
by Hawthorne. Life went by now very happily, a quiet evening with his wife "being more musical than any opera." Children were born into Craigie House: Charles, about whom he
wrote his *Ode to a Child;* Ernest; Fanny, who died early,
and for whom he wrote his *Resignation.*

Every evening the wife read aloud to him; now Shelley
(whose poetry, he said, "meets and satisfies certain moods
more than any other"), Milton, Heine, Ruskin, and a num-
berless list from Spanish, French, Danish, and German literatures. "Books," he said, "are in fact the cheapest of all our
pleasures."

With his poor eyes, he worked as much as he was able, and
then frolicked with his children. Now, as he records in his
journal, he "dragged Charles on his new sled over snow and
ice in the garden, to his great delight," or made snow houses
in the front yard, or cast lead flatirons for them, or wrote
letters that they might find them under their pillows.

When *Evangeline* was published, in 1847, the musical
hexameters met with the heartiest reception.

Then followed the *Golden Legend,* the central thread being the story of Prince Henry as told by Hartmann Von der
Aue, a Minnesinger of the twelfth century.

College duties had become irksome to Longfellow—"not
so much the labor, but the going round and round in the
tread-mill," and the poet resigned in 1854, after eighteen years
of service, to be succeeded by James Russell Lowell.

Hiawatha was published the following year, and made a
decided sensation. Everybody read:

> At the door on summer evenings,
> Sat the little Hiawatha;
> Heard the whispering of the pine-trees,
> Sounds of music, words of wonder;

In a month ten thousand copies had been sold, and in a year and a half, fifty thousand copies.

In 1858 *The Courtship of Miles Standish* appeared, and twenty-five thousand were disposed of the first week. Truly fame had come. Nothing seemed wanting to make life complete, when, lo! like a thunderbolt out of a clear sky, the tragedy of his life came.

On July 9, 1861, Mrs. Longfellow was sealing up some curls which she had just cut from the heads of her little daughters. Her thin dress caught fire from a lighted match, and, before her husband could rescue her, she was burned fatally, dying the next morning. She was buried on the anniversary of her wedding-day, in Mount Auburn.

He wrote in his journal two months afterward, "How can I live any longer! . . . The glimmer of golden leaves in the sunshine . . . everything without, full of loveliness. But within me the hunger, the famine of the heart." To a friend he wrote, "To the eyes of others, outwardly, calm; but inwardly bleeding to death." Two years afterward he says, in his journal, "The burden seems too great for me to bear."

For twenty years he lived on and did his beautiful work, finding consolation in his children, but the sorrow was never healed. Two years before his death, he wrote, and put away in his portfolio, these touching lines:

THE CROSS OF SNOW

> In the long sleepless watches of the night,
> A gentle face—the face of one long dead—
> Looks at me from the wall, where round its head

The night-lamp casts a halo of pale light.
Here in this room she died; and soul more white
    Never through martyrdom of fire was led
    To its repose; nor can in books be read
    The legend of a life more benedight.
There is a mountain in the distant West
    That, sun-defying, in its deep ravines
    Displays a cross of snow upon its side;
Such is the cross I wear upon my breast
    These eighteen years, through all the changing scenes
    And seasons, changeless since the day she died.

During the Civil War another tragic blow befell the poet.
For his son Charles, fighting with the cavalry in the Army
of the Potomac, fell in action and nearly died of his wounds.

Seven years after his wife's death, in 1868, Longfellow made
his last visit to Europe, taking his three daughters with him.
Tales of a Wayside Inn, the *New England Tragedies* (for
which he read over a hundred volumes), and *Dante's Divine
Comedy,* in translation, had been published, and he had
earned a rest. Cambridge University conferred upon him
the degree of Doctor of Laws, as his own Cambridge had
done. Oxford University also gave him the degree of D.C.L.
He breakfasted with Gladstone, the Duke of Argyle, and other
leading men, and went to Windsor Castle at the request of
Queen Victoria. He spent two days with Tennyson in the Isle
of Wight, and saw Liszt in Rome, who set to music the in-
troduction to the *Golden Legend.* After eighteen months he
returned to his home and to his work.

At the fiftieth anniversary of his class at Bowdoin College
he read his *Morituri Salutamus,* an allusion to the gladiators,
who thus accosted a Roman Emperor when they were about
to engage in combat before him,—"We who are about to
die salute you"; a beautiful poem showing

> How far the gulf-stream of our youth may flow
> Into the arctic regions of our lives.

When he was seventy-two came a lovely present from the school children of Cambridge, an armchair made from wood of the horse chestnut tree under which the Village Blacksmith stood. The poem written for them was given to every child who came to see and sit in the chair.

In 1880 *Ultima Thule* was published, and the world knew that the last things were being said before the final journey.

That year fifteen thousand school children of Cincinnati celebrated the poet's birthday with recitations from his poems and singing of his songs. He wrote them to "live up to the best that is in them, so that their monument may be that of Euripides:

" 'This monument does not make thee famous, O Euripides, but thou makest the monument famous.' "

Each summer he spent at his home at Nahant, by the ocean, a two-story light-brown house, with a broad piazza on all sides. In August of 1880, on the eve of a long stay abroad, I took my only child to see the noble man. Longfellow, with a tenderness natural to him, put both hands upon the boy's shoulders, told him what he must learn in Germany, and took him to see the yacht of his son Charles, lying at anchor at the foot of his grounds.

His last acts of kindness were to children. On March 18 four schoolboys came from Boston to see him, and to ask for his autograph, which he cheerfully gave. Six days later, on March 24, 1882, having taken a severe cold, with his dear ones all about him, he sank quietly to rest.

Longfellow's leaving of this life has an analogy in his own *Nature*, which one critic has called "one of the choicest sonnets in any language":

As a fond mother, when the day is o'er,
  Leads by the hand her little child to bed,
  Half willing, half reluctant to be led,
And leave his broken playthings on the floor,
Still gazing at them through the open door,
  Nor wholly reassured and comforted
  By promises of others in their stead,
  Which, though more splendid, may not please him more;
So Nature deals with us, and takes away
  Our playthings one by one, and by the hand
  Leads us to rest so gently, that we go
Scarce knowing if we wish to go or stay,
  Being too full of sleep to understand
  How far the unknown transcends the what we know.

Longfellow was an untiring and careful worker, usually employing the mornings in composition, and taking his exercise in walking, sometimes ten miles, at sunrise or sunset, when he could enjoy the sublime beauties of nature. Conversant with many languages, a polished scholar, he yet wrote so simply that everybody could understand. He was the true singer, combining the art of rhythm with the heart of song. Nearly all of his works have been translated into German and French, and several into Swedish, Dutch, Danish, Italian, Portuguese, Spanish, Polish, and Russian. *The Psalm of Life* has been translated into Chinese, Maráthi, Sanskrit, Latin, and Hebrew. Nearly a million volumes of his collected poems have been sold in America.

His words on Charles Sumner well apply to him:

Were a star quenched on high,
  For ages would its light,
Still travelling downward from the sky,
  Shine on our mortal sight.

> So when a great man dies,
>   For years beyond our ken
> The light he leaves behind him lies
>   Upon the paths of men.

His marble image stands in Westminster Abbey, in the Poet's Corner; but, better still, he lives in the hearts of the people of two hemispheres. The ambition of youth, "I will be eminent," was realized, though he was never satisfied with his labors. He said, "Authors and artists of every kind have one element of unhappiness in their lot, namely, the disproportion between their designs and their deeds. Even the greatest cannot execute one tenth part of what they conceive."

Of how few can be said what has been said of Longfellow, that "he not only wrote no line which, dying, he would wish to blot, but not one which, living, he had not a right to be proud of."

He helped to realize for humanity the last words which he ever penned:

> Out of the shadow of night
> The world moves into light;
> It is daybreak everywhere!

John Greenleaf Whittier

The world, O Father! hath not wronged
With loss the life by thee prolonged;
But still, with every added year,
More beautiful thy works appear!

As thou hast made thy world without,
  Make thou more fair my world within;
Shine through its lingering clouds of doubt;
  Rebuke its haunting shapes of sin;

Fill, brief or long, my granted span
Of life with love to thee and man;
Strike when thou wilt the hour of rest,
But let my last days be my best!

THUS wrote Whittier in 1868 in his poem, *The Clear Vision,* when he was sixty-one years old. He had his wish; his last days were indeed his best. He died on the morning of September 7, 1892, at the age of eighty-four, the most loved poet in America. Bells were tolled in many places, and public buildings and schoolhouses lowered their flags to half-mast.

His life began in poverty; it ended in comfort and renown. The barefoot boy became one of the great humanitarian leaders of the age.

John Greenleaf Whittier was born on December 17, 1807, in an oldfashioned farmhouse, three miles northeast of Haverhill, Mass. "The building," says W. Sloane Kennedy in his life of the poet, "is believed to be considerably over two hundred years old, in as wild and lonely a place as Craigen-puttock,—the hills shutting down all around, so that there is absolutely no prospect in any direction, and no other house visible. . . . Between the front door of the old homestead and the road rises a grassy, wooded bank, at the foot of which flows a little amber-colored brook."

This brook was dear to the farmer boy, for he says in *Snow-Bound,*

> We minded that the sharpest ear
> The buried brooklet could not hear,
> The music of whose liquid lip
> Had been to us companionship,
> And, in our lonely life, had grown
> To have an almost human tone.

In the plain Whittier home were John, the father, an upright, hard-working farmer, a decisive man of few words; Abigail Hussey, the mother, a woman of great and devoted piety; and four children, Mary, John, Matthew, and Elizabeth.

The boys worked on the farm, and the girls helped the mother in her household duties, which were many, besides the spinning and weaving of linen and woolen cloth for the family.

The quiet, uneventful life of the Whittier household had much of hard work in it, and at the same time much of real happiness.

In *Snow-Bound,* the poet writes:

> Meanwhile we did our nightly chores,—
> Brought in the wood from out of doors,
> Littered the stalls, and from the mows
> Raked down the herd's grass for the cows;
> Heard the horse whinneying for his corn;
> And, sharply clashing horn on horn,
> Impatient down the stanchion rows
> The cattle shake their walnut bows.

In *The Barefoot Boy* there is a charming picture of this early life of simple pleasures:

> I was rich in flowers and trees,
> Humming-birds and honey-bees;
> For my sport the squirrel played,
> Plied the snouted mole his spade;
> For my taste the blackberry cone
> Purpled over hedge and stone;
> Laughed the brook for my delight
> Through the day and through the night,
> Whispering at the garden wall,
> Talked with me from fall to fall;
> Mine the sand-rimmed pickerel pond,
> Mine the walnut slopes beyond,
> Mine, on bending orchard trees,
> Apples of Hesperides!
>
> .   .   .   .   .
>
> O for festal dainties spread,
> Like my bowl of milk and bread,—
> Pewter spoon and bowl of wood,
> On the door-stone, gray and rude!
> O'er me, like a regal tent,
> Cloudy-ribbed, the sunset bent,
> Purple-curtained, fringed with gold,

> Looped in many a wind-swung fold;
> While for music came the play
> Of the pied frogs' orchestra;
>
> .   .   .   .   .   .
>
> I was monarch: pomp and joy
> Waited on the barefoot boy!

There was little in Farmer Whittier's home to awaken thirst for knowledge. The books numbered about twenty, most of them journals and memoirs of pious Quakers. Bunyan's *Pilgrim's Progress,* a soiled pamphlet on a *Wicked Dancing-Party in New Jersey,* and a *Life of David,* gave some variety to the Quaker memoirs. The principal reading, aside from the weekly newspaper and the almanac, was the Bible, which the good mother read to her children, and conversed with them familiarly about it.

When the poet was fourteen years of age, a wandering peddler sang to him some of the songs of Burns; and Joshua Coffin, his first schoolmaster, loaned him a volume of Burns's poems. "This was about the first poetry I had ever read (with the exception of that of the Bible, of which I had been a close student)," said Whittier, years afterward, "and it had a lasting influence upon me."

He at once, he says, "began to make rhymes," and when a small lad he is said to have composed poems on his slate, instead of using it for his arithmetic.

He was encouraged in his writing by his sister Mary, who, when he was nineteen, sent one of his poems, *The Deity,* to the *Newburyport Free Press,* conducted by William Lloyd Garrison, then only twenty-two years of age.

The farmer boy waited anxiously to see his poem in print, but the weeks went by and it did not appear. Finally, one day the postman rode past with his saddlebags, and threw out the newspaper to young Whittier, who was mending fences with his Uncle Moses.

The youth opened the sheet, and to his astonishment found *The Deity* in the *Poet's Corner*. He was so dazed as well as overjoyed, that his uncle had to call him several times to his work, before he seemed conscious that he was engaged in such earthly pursuits as mending stone fences.

He sent other poems which were accepted, though of course not paid for. Finally, Garrison decided to ride fifteen miles on horseback to see this new contributor, whose poems he liked.

The poet was in the cornfield working, without coat or shoes—having on only a shirt, pantaloons, and straw hat. He hastened to make himself as presentable as possible, and shyly met the young reformer.

The father was called in, and Garrison urged that his son be sent to school, as he had superior abilities. But the elder Whittier remonstrated "against putting such notions in his son's head."

However, the advice was heeded, and, grateful that someone appreciated and praised his work, the youth determined to educate himself. A young man who worked on the Whittier farm summers added to his small income by making ladies' slippers and shoes during the winters. He offered to teach the poet his trade, and the offer was gladly accepted. The result was enough money earned to buy a suit of clothes, and to pay for board and tuition for six months at the Haverhill Academy, besides a twenty-five cent piece which he always carried, so as to have money in his pocket.

Whittier studied the ordinary English books, took lessons in French, and gave especial attention to history. He boarded with the editor and publisher of the *Haverhill Gazette*, A. W. Thayer, whose wife remembered the youth with "tall,

erect figure, ready wit, perfect courtesy, and infallible sense
of truth and justice."

A daughter of Judge Minot wrote F. H. Underwood for
his life of the poet: "Whittier was a very handsome, distin-
guished-looking young man. His eyes were remarkably beautiful. He was always kind to children, and under a very grave
and quiet exterior there was a real love of fun, and a keen
sense of the ludicrous. With intimate friends he talked a great
deal, and in a wonderfully interesting manner; usually earnest, often analytical, and frequently playful. . . . The study
of human nature was very interesting to him, and his insight
was keen. . . . He was very modest, never conceited, never
egotistic. . . . He was exceedingly conscientious. He cared
for people—quite as much for the plainest and most unculti-
vated, if they were original and had something in them, as
for the most polished. . . . He had a retentive memory and
a marvellous store of information on many subjects. I once
saw a little commonplace book of his, full of quaint things,
and as interesting as Southey's."

At the close of the school term Whittier taught the district
school in West Amesbury, and earned enough money to pay
for board and tuition for another six months at the Academy.

The schooling was now over, necessarily, and, like his "barefoot boy,"

> All too soon these feet must hide
> In the prison cells of pride,
> Lose the freedom of the sod,
> Like a colt's for work be shod,
> Made to tread the mills of toil,
> Up and down in ceaseless moil.

Through the influence of Garrison, he passed the winter
of 1828 in Boston, writing for the *American Manufacturer*,

a protectionist organ, receiving nine dollars a week for his services. He returned to the farm in June, and remained there for a year, writing much, both in prose and poetry. During a part of this time he edited the *Haverhill Gazette,* and wrote for the *New England Weekly Review,* published at Hartford, Conn.

He "issued proposals to publish a 'History of Haverhill,' in one volume at eighty-seven and a half cents per copy," but nobody seemed desirous of spending so much money for a book, and this project was abandoned.

His articles had found favor with the *Review,* of which George D. Prentice was the editor, and when the latter went to Kentucky to found the Louisville *Courier-Journal,* he suggested that young Whittier be asked to take his place. Whittier received his invitation to take the editorship while at work on the farm. He said, "I could not have been more utterly astonished if I had been told that I was appointed minister to the great Khan of Tartary."

He remained editor of the *Review* for nearly two years, writing over forty poems for it, besides prose articles.

When Whittier was twenty-four his first book was published by Hammer & Phelps, Hartford, Conn., *Legends of New England,* sketches in prose and verse. The next year he edited the *Literary Remains of J. G. C. Brainard,* a gifted young friend, and a year later published at his own expense *Justice and Expediency; or, Slavery considered with a View to its Rightful and Effective Remedy, Abolition.*

Meantime Whittier's father had died, and the poet returned to the farm to help support the family. He says, "I worked hard to make both ends meet; and, aided by my mother's and sister's thrift and economy, in some measure succeeded."

The pamphlet on slavery of course provoked opposition, but Lewis Tappan of New York was so pleased with the ardent spirit and unanswerable logic of the booklet, that he issued gratuitously ten thousand copies.

The young poet, with laudable literary ambition and political ambition as well, knew fully how he was hedging up his way to success, by becoming the champion of this hated cause. He and his friend Garrison had joined hands to rise or fall together.

He was chosen a delegate to the National Anti-Slavery Convention at Philadelphia, December 4–6, 1833, and was one of the secretaries. Garrison sat up all night in the attic of a colored man to draft the Declaration of Principles, which Whittier and others signed. Whittier said, years afterward, "I set a higher value on my name as appended to the Anti-Slavery Declaration of 1833 than on the title-page of any book." He wrote in the next few years his burning *Voices of Freedom,* which stirred many hearts all over the country.

The *Slave-Ship,* was a pitiful story of a shipload of slaves who sailed from Bonny in Africa, April, 1819, and who, having been made blind by a contagious disease and thereby rendered unsalable, were thrown, thirty-six of them, into the sea and drowned. This story too thrilled the hearts of all lovers of humanity.

In 1838 Whittier became the editor of the *Pennsylvania Freeman,* an organ of the Anti-Slavery Society. The office of the paper in Philadelphia was sacked and burned by a mob, and the poet's health failing, he returned to Massachusetts. The farm, meantime, had been sold, and his mother, aunt, and sister had moved to Amesbury that they might be near the Friends' Meeting House. Whittier joined them, and Amesbury was his legal home till his death.

Those years were full of labor and much obloquy. Several times Whittier was mobbed, and his life endangered. Once when he and George Thompson, the noted abolitionist, escaped from an angry mob of five hundred, though they were hurt by the sticks and stones, the poet said, "We did not much fear death, but we did dread gross personal indignities."

Notwithstanding his unpopular anti-slavery views, he was elected to the State Legislature in 1835, and in 1836, by the citizens of Haverhill, but declined a reelection in 1837. In 1844 Whittier edited the *Middlesex Standard,* a Liberty party paper. The poet said, "I early saw the necessity of separate political action, and was one of the founders of the Liberty party—the germ of the present Republican party." Later, for a time, he was an associate editor of the *National Era* at Washington, the paper in which *Uncle Tom's Cabin* appeared as a serial. Above eighty of Whittier's poems were published in the *Era* from 1847 to 1859.

His pen seemed never idle. He knew New England history by heart, and used it as Tennyson used the early legends of his country in the *Idylls of the King.* His ballads soon became dear to the people.

The years passed quietly and happily away at the Amesbury home, a plain two-story house with many forest trees in front of it. The poet's study was simple, with its open book-shelves holding several hundred volumes, and its cheery Franklin stove with its wood fire, which Whittier himself always cared for. With him lived his mother who died in 1857, after she had seen her son come to fame, and Elizabeth, the youngest sister, also a poet, who died in the autumn of 1864.

In his *Yankee Gypsies,* Whittier tells this incident of his mother:

> On one occasion, a few years ago, on my return from the field at evening, I was told that a foreigner had asked for lodgings during the night, but that, influenced by his dark, repulsive appearance, my mother had very reluctantly refused his request.
>
> I found her by no means satisfied with her decision. "What

if a son of mine was in a strange land?" she inquired, self-reproachfully. Greatly to her relief, I volunteered to go in pursuit of the wanderer, and, taking a crosspath over the fields, soon overtook him. He had just been rejected at the house of our nearest neighbor, and was standing in a state of dubious perplexity in the street.

His looks quite justified my mother's suspicions. He was an olive-complexioned, black-bearded Italian, with an eye like a live coal, such a face as perchance looks out on the traveller in the passes of the Abruzzi—one of those bandit-visages which Salvator painted.

With some difficulty I gave him to understand my errand, when he overwhelmed me with thanks, and joyfully followed me back. He took his seat with us at the suppertable; and when we were all gathered around the hearth that cold autmnal evening, he told us, partly by words and partly by gestures, the story of his life and misfortunes, amused us with descriptions of the grape-gatherings and festivals of his sunny clime, edified my mother with a recipe for making bread of chestnuts; and in the morning when, after breakfast, his dark sullen face lighted up, and his fierce eye moistened with grateful emotion as in his own silvery Tuscan accent he poured out his thanks, we marvelled at the fears which had so nearly closed our doors against him; and, as he departed, we all felt that he had left with us the blessing of the poor.

Whittier has immortalized his sister Elizabeth in *Snow-Bound.*

> Upon the motley braided mat
> Our youngest and our dearest sat,
> Lifting her large, sweet, asking eyes,
> Now bathed within the fadeless green
> And holy peace of Paradise.

For some years after the death of Whittier's mother and sister, a favorite niece, the daughter of his brother Matthew, lived with him, and at her marriage the poet went to live with some cousins at Oak Knoll, Danvers, a beautiful home in the midst of sixty acres of well-kept lawn, flower beds, and forest trees, all carefully tended. He still retained his Amesbury house, making it his legal residence.

A few years before Mr. Whittier's death, I saw him in this attractive home, surrounded by his books, his pet birds, and his dogs. The mockingbird so much enjoyed joining in our conversation, that the poet was obliged to cover his cage, so that we could hear each other talk. One of his dogs came and held up a bruised paw to me for sympathy.

Mr. Whittier's eyes were as dark and handsome as ever, and his smile as benignant, and often merry. "I have got a great deal out of life; more than most people," he said. "I try to remember only the bright and good—I have forgotten all the mischief done." As though he of whom Longfellow wrote,

> Whose daily life anticipates
> The life to come, and in whose thought and word
> The spiritual world preponderates,

could have done any mischief ever!

Mrs. Harriet Prescott Spofford gave this picture of Whittier at his Danvers home:

He is out of doors a great deal. He takes pleasure in the horses, and is a fine and fearless driver, and when there is nothing else to do, he watches from his portico the antics of the dogs and squirrels, the latter (as no guns are allowed upon the place) taking liberties that puzzle such fellows as the little Dandie Dinmont, who has the care of the house upon his shoulders, and who darts after them in a terrible fury, and when he has treed them, in his wrath stands on his hind feet, waves his paws and whines, begging them to come down. In winter some of the squirrels come to the windows to be fed; and the quails and bluebirds are quite as tame at all times.

An incident given in the *Literary World* for December, 1877, illustrates the same kindness of heart in the poet which characterized his mother. The writer says:

> When I was a young man, trying to get an education, I went about the country peddling sewing-silk to help myself through college; and one Saturday night found me at Amesbury, a stranger, and without a lodging-place. It happened that the first house at which I called was Whittier's, and he himself came to the door. On hearing my request he said he was very sorry that he could not keep me, but it was quarterly meeting, and his house was full. He, however, took the trouble to show me to a neighbor's, where he left me; but that did not seem wholly to suit his idea of hospitality, for in the course of the evening he made his appearance, saying that it had occurred to him that he could sleep on a lounge, and give up his own bed to me, which it is, perhaps, needless to say was not allowed.
>
> But this was not all. The next morning he came again, with the suggestion that I might perhaps like to attend meeting, inviting me to go with him; and he gave me a seat next to himself. The meeting lasted an hour, during which there was not a word spoken by any one. We all sat in silence that length of time, then all arose, shook hands, and dispersed; and I remember it as one of the best meetings I ever attended.

Almost yearly a book of poems appeared from Whittier's pen. His health was so poor that for some years he could not write over a half-hour at a time, on account of headache, brought on by overwork in his early days of journalism, and yet, like Charles Darwin, he accomplished more than most men with perfect health. He saved his time, going little into society, yet, was always gracious about sending his autograph to those who asked it, cordial in seeing those who called upon him, and helped scores of young writers, reading their manuscripts, and asking for their publication in periodicals. "It is easy," said Whittier, "to tear a volume in pieces by criticism, but I try to find its merits."

After *Snow-Bound*, published in 1866, which had an exceptional popularity, the *Tent on the Beach*, 1867, became the favorite book among the nearly forty published by the poet, a few of these being collections of poetry for children, and hymns, and one historical novel, *Margaret Smith's Journal*.

In the *Tent on the Beach*, Whittier and two friends, Bayard Taylor and James T. Fields, are represented as encamped on Salisbury Beach, with the Isles of Shoals on one side and Boar's Head on the other. Each person is supposed to tell some tale of the olden time. *The Wreck of Rivermouth, Kallundborg Church*, and *The Dead Ship of Harpswell* are perhaps the best of these charming tales. The latter is as weird as *The Wreck of the Hesperus*, and the language is singularly suited to the thought.

While deeply interested in politics, and in all matters of state, Whittier was more than all else a devotedly religious man—not given to creeds, but a close follower of his Lord. *The Eternal Goodness* shows the spirit of the man, and is often quoted, both for its poetic beauty and its childlike trust:

> I know not what the future hath
> Of marvel or surprise,
> Assured alone that life and death
> His mercy underlies.

>   •   •   •   •   •

> I know not where His islands lift
> Their fronded palms in air;
> I only know I cannot drift
> Beyond His love and care.

He was a bitter foe to intolerance, never forgetting the treatment received by the Quakers, as shown in the spirited poems *Barclay of Ury, Cassandra Southwick, The King's Missive,* and others. Much of Whittier's work will last—indeed, is already a part of our American life and history. *Barbara Frietchie* will be read as long as the story of our Civil War interests a freed and united nation.

Some of Whittier's poems have been translated into the German language, and *The Cry of a Lost Soul* into Portuguese by the Emperor of Brazil, who met the poet and greatly admired him.

When Whittier was seventy years old, on December 17, 1877, the publishers of the *Atlantic Monthly* gave a dinner to the poet at Hotel Brunswick, in Boston, Emerson, Longfellow, Holmes, Howells, and other authors being present. During his remaining years his birthday was always remembered by gifts and gatherings at his home, and celebrations among school children in many cities.

Whittier was always an advocate of suffrage for woman. He said, "I have no fear that man will be less manly or woman less womanly when they meet on terms of equality before the law. . . . Stronger than statutes or conventions, she will be conservative of all that the true man loves and honors in woman."

The beloved Quaker poet's last years were peaceful, surrounded by his friends and neighbors, and the scenes he had loved all his life.

At his death in 1892 he left, it is estimated, over a hundred and twenty-two thousand dollars, accumulated by his copyrights, to his relatives, to the Amesbury and Salisbury Home for Aged Women, to a hospital in Newburyport, and to the Normal and Agricultural Institute for Colored and Indian Pupils at Hampton, Va.

He left to the world, not only his poems, but an inspiring record of manhood, worthy of emulation. From the farm and the shoe-shop, never complaining of his surroundings, he conquered success.

Edgar Allan Poe

EDGAR ALLAN POE was, perhaps, one of the most brilliant writers who ever lived. His writings, however, belong to a different sphere from those of Longfellow, Lowell, Whittier, Holmes, Bryant, or Emerson. They wrote from the realms of nature, joy, happiness, hope, ease. Poe spoke from the dungeon of depression. He was in constant struggle with poverty, and his whole life was a tragedy. Yet,

> By a route obscure and lonely,
> Haunted by ill angels only,

he became one of the world's eminent poets. He was not always and everywhere recognized as great. It was, indeed, not in his own country, but in France that his poetry received its most generous appreciation. Mallarmé, Rimbaud, Verlaine, and the French Symbolist poets first realized that his own lines might well be applied to himself as poet and singer.

> None sing so wildly well
> As the angel Israfel,

> And the giddy stars (so legends tell)
> Ceasing their hymns, attend the spell
> Of his voice, all mute.

And it was they who exploited his poetic subject matter and his highly subjective mood. It was they, too, who understood his particular technical skill in versification and attempted to imitate it, bringing revolutionary innovations to their poetry.

In America and England Poe has, of course, long been recognized for his skill as a short story writer. It was he who was responsible, in stories like *The Purloined Letter,* for the invention of the modern detective story. Sherlock Holmes and Watson are patterned on his models. From them come a whole line of police inspectors, detectives, and "private eyes."

It is not the detective story alone that Poe has fathered. He is a master of mystery and horror, and he has made tales of the supernatural or the fantastic seem real by application of convincing detail. His method is one of intensification. The result is tales bizarre and grotesque, yet convincing. He controls his exaggeration, as in his description of the simoon in *MS Found in a Bottle,* so that we continue to believe. Skeptically questioning his own fabrications, he persuades us that they are real when he answers the questions he has raised. His stories usually begin with a bang. *The Pit and the Pendulum* starts with "the dread sentence of death," and *The Cask of Amontillado* with a thousand personal injuries and a vow of revenge. Our interest aroused, it is held by the suspense which Poe is able to sustain through an entire story. So skilfully does he manage these devices that we hardly miss the characters whom he is unable to create. His stick-like figures are borne along on a wave of suspense, horror or mystery, and we get lost in their predicaments and do not think of questioning them.

Poe was born in Boston on February 19, 1809. His father was a Marylander. His grandfather, also from Maryland, had been a distinguished revolutionary soldier and a friend of Lafayette. Later in life, however, a hereditary family weakness resulted in the madness of the old man. Poe's parents were both actors, who toured the country, always moving and continuously on the verge of poverty. His father, a man of extremely unstable character, drank heavily. Before his wife died, in Virginia, at the early age of twenty-four, he had abandoned her and their three children. Two of the children were adopted by immediate friends of the family upon the mother's death, for the father had disappeared without a trace. Mr. John Allan, a rich tobacco merchant of the city, took Edgar and insisted upon calling him Edgar *Allan* Poe. His wife was childless and young Edgar, a boy "both beautiful and precocious," filled a need in their lives. Or perhaps he merely served to keep Mrs. Allan occupied and her attention off her husband. For despite the rigidly repressive code which he visited on young Edgar in the name of Calvin and religion, he was a hypocritical philanderer who produced three illegitimate children while he lectured young Edgar about sin.

While still a boy young Edgar was sent abroad for a year to an English school. Though the school was probably chosen for its ability to impress the Allan neighbors rather than for the excellence of its instruction, Poe did learn something there. Freed from the narrowness of his foster parent's home, he was made aware of the poetry of Byron for the first time by his fellow students. And Byron's poetry had a marked influence upon the boy.

When Poe returned to America, he was sent to the Richmond Academy and later to the University of Virginia, a liberal institution for young Southern aristocrats. Free once again from the exacting rule of his foster father, Poe began to sow his wild oats. Not that he sowed many. Though Mr. Allan had sent the boy to a college attended by wealthy young men, he refused to supply him with even a modest amount of money. Since Poe had been gambling and living, for the first time, rather freely, a break was inevitable. And when young Miss Royster, with whom he had been romancing, married someone else, Poe left college and enlisted in the army.

Much has been written about Poe's unstable character. And both his later years and his hereditary make-up point to a serious flaw in his personality. It should be pointed out, however, that the young man rose, without assistance, in the ranks, becoming a Sergeant-Major before buying himself out of the service. Afterward, he felt it necessary to justify himself as "an officer and a gentleman" before the snobbish Richmond circle of his foster parents. He asked Mr. Allan to request an appointment to West Point for him, and his foster father reluctantly and coolly complied.

Poe, who had been a brilliant student at college, left for West Point hoping to take an accelerated course so that he could spend his spare time writing. Unfortunately, he was disappointed in his expectations. Moreover, the rigid discipline of the Military Academy irked him. In his second year, he decided to leave. His court-martial and expulsion were not the result of a moral fault, as some writers have assumed. Poe decided to breach the rules deliberately and absented himself from required chapel attendance in order to hasten his departure from a place that was odious to him in every way.

Poe went to live with an aunt, Mrs. Clemm, upon his release from West Point. He had already published three volumes of poetry—*Tamerlane* (1827), *Al Aaraaf* (1829), and *Poems* (1831). Now he decided to try his hand at fiction. While living with Mrs. Clemm, in Baltimore, he entered a prize competition and won fifty dollars for a short story called *MS Found in a Bottle*. This was enough to convince him that he should devote his life to literature, and when he was offered a job as editor of the *Southern Literary Messenger,* he accepted immediately and left for Richmond in the summer of 1835.

Poe did well by the *Messenger.* He was a good editor, and before he left he had raised the circulation from five hundred to thirty-five hundred copies and made the magazine nationally known. Confident of his own ability, he was distressed by news from his aunt. She and her young daughter were practically indigent. Poe had already professed his love for his young cousin, but as she was not yet fourteen, plans for the future had not been discussed. Now Poe pleaded with his aunt to allow them to marry at once. Accordingly, on May 16, 1836, the twenty-seven-year-old Poe and his young cousin were married. The following February the young couple, accompanied by Mrs. Clemm, left for the greener pastures of New York.

Poe was disappointed with New York and he soon left it for Philadelphia, a city that shared honors with the larger one as a publishing center. There Poe soon found work as a literary critic and editor. His first job was as an associate editor of William E. Burton's *Gentleman's Magazine.* Later he became editor of *Graham's Magazine,* a distinguished publication whose circulation rose from five thousand to forty thousand copies under Poe's skilful direction. Furthermore, Poe's short stories and incisive literary criticism had by this time won him a wide reputation.

Trouble was preparing, however. In January, 1842, the first blow fell. Poe's wife, Virginia, suffered a severe hemorrhage. The ensuing events are best told in Poe's own words. He says, in a letter written later:

Six years ago, a wife, whom I loved as no man ever loved before, ruptured a blood vessel in singing. Her life was despaired
of. I took leave of her forever and underwent all the agonies of
her death. She recovered partially and I again hoped. At the
end of a year the vessel broke again—I went through precisely
the same scene. Again in about a year afterward. Then again
—again—again and even once again at varying intervals. Each
time I felt all the agonies of her death—and at each accession
of the disorder I loved her more dearly and clung to her life
with more desperate pertinacity. But I am constitutionally
sensitive—nervous in a very unusual degree. I became insane,
with long intervals of horrible sanity. During these fits of abso-
lute unconsciousness I drank . . .

There were, of course, intervals during which Virginia's
health improved. But gradually, she sank. And her husband
sank too. He continued to write. As a matter of fact, it was
during this period that he wrote *The Gold Bug,* one of his
most famous stories, winning one hundred dollars for it in a
prize competition. But the effects of drink and anxiety over
Virginia's condition made him unreliable. He was soon forced
to leave the editor's chair at *Graham's,* though he continued
to contribute stories and reviews to that magazine.

In 1837, hoping that a change of scene would help both of
them, Poe took his wife back to New York. He soon got work
with the *Evening Mirror* and continued writing poems, stories,
and reviews. His literary criticism was particularly caustic, and
it earned him some lifelong enemies. However, despite some
literary feuding, Poe did rather well. Later, seeing a better
opportunity, he transferred his activity from the *Mirror* to
the *Broadway News.* And in 1845 the versatile writer published both a book of *Tales* and one containing *The Raven
and other Poems.*

In the year that Poe published his two books he also realized
a lifelong ambition. He became proprietor as well as editor

of the *Broadway Journal*, his former employers having sold out. This event was another stroke of ill luck in disguise. For Poe had no capital, and despite his skill and the fifteen hour work days that he put in at the magazine, it soon collapsed. The Poes were reduced to poverty, and even in the small cottage which they took at Fordham—then thirteen miles out in the country—they could not make ends meet.

It was in this cottage at Fordham that the heaviest blow of all fell. Here, in January, 1846, Poe's young wife died. A friend recalls the scene, as, in the depth of winter, "She lay on a straw bed, wrapped in her husband's great coat, with a large tortoise-shell cat in her bosom. The wonderful cat seemed conscious of her great usefulness. The coat and the cat were the sufferer's only means of warmth, except as her husband held her hands, and her mother her feet." Small wonder that the poet, witnessing such a scene, was driven to complete despair. For, as he tells us in *Annabel Lee,* a poem written in memory of his wife:

> . . . our love it was stronger by far than the love
>   Of those who were older than we;
>   Of many far wiser than we;
> And neither the angels in heaven above,
>   Nor the demons down under the sea,
> Can ever dissever my soul from the soul
>   Of the beautiful Annabel Lee.
>
> For the moon never beams without bringing me dreams
>   Of the beautiful Annabel Lee:
> And the stars never rise, but I feel the bright eyes
>   Of the beautiful Annabel Lee:
> So all the night-tide, I lie down by the side
> Of my darling—my darling—my life and my bride
>   In the sepulcher there by the sea,
>   In her tomb by the sounding sea.

Poe was completely broken at the death of his wife. He might be describing his own life at this time when he says,

> The play is the tragedy *Man,*
> And its hero the Conqueror Worm.

Drink was his surest means of escape from his sorrows, and he took to it. But he was able to rouse himself even from the depths of his despair now and then. *The Bells,* which has been called "one of the most successful verbal imitations of sound in the English language," was written at this time. Its effect is secured largely, as has been pointed out, through the skilful contrast of close vowel sounds,

> How they tinkle, tinkle, tinkle
> In the icy air of night.

And open vowel sounds,

> Hear the mellow wedding bells,
> Golden bells.

And the poem seems to be filled with the jangling

> Of the bells, bells, bells
> Of the bells, bells, bells, bells
> Bells, bells, bells—
> . . . the rhyming and the chiming of the bells!

Now Poe sought consolation for his tragic loss in the friendship of Mrs. Whitman, a fellow poet. There were even plans for a marriage. But it did not come off. Later he was to find solace in his friendship with Mrs. Richmond, the "Annie" to whom he exclaims,

> Thank Heaven! the crisis—
> The danger is past,
> And the lingering illness
> Is over at last—

And the fever called "Living"
 Is conquered at last.
Sadly I know
 I am shorn of my strength,
And no muscle I move
 As I lie at full length—
But no matter!—I feel
 I am better at length.

And, indeed, "the fever called 'Living'" was almost over. On returning from a lecture tour that had taken him back to Richmond, Poe stopped off in Baltimore. He was ill and depressed, and apparently—accounts of his last days differ—he had been drinking. On October 3, 1849, he was found, unconscious, before a polling place on a Baltimore street. An election had taken place that day, and it has been assumed that Poe had been plied with drugged liquor and taken from one polling place to another to be voted as a "repeater." Such corrupt practices were not uncommon in those days. Perhaps it was in such a sordid way that Poe met his end. But we shall never know. For Poe regained only partial consciousness and could not account for his condition before he breathed his last, toward five o'clock in the morning of Sunday, October 7. "The tragedy *Man*" had been played out.

Oliver Wendell Holmes

I N the summer of 1886, Dr. Holmes, nearing the borderline of the eighties, sailed for Europe. At Liverpool, as he landed, he was met by a delegation of some of the most prominent persons in Europe,—authors, physicians, men of social position and political power. In London he met such men as the Dukes of Argyll and Westminster, Lord Napier, Robert Browning, and John Ruskin. He visited at 10 Downing Street, in the offices of the then Prime Minister, the famous William E. Gladstone.

Archdeacon Farrar spent two hours in showing him about Westminster Abbey. He dined with Mr. Peel, Speaker of the House of Commons. In Dr. Holmes's charming reminiscences of his journey, *Our Hundred Days in Europe,* in the *Atlantic Monthly,* he says: "I had the pleasure of dining with the distinguished Mr. Bryce, whose acquaintance I made in our own country, through my son, who has introduced me to many agreeable persons of his own generation, with whose companionship I am glad to mend the broken and mere fragmentary circle of old friendships."

He visited Tennyson at his home in the Isle of Wight. At Cambridge University he received the degree of Doctor of Laws, and the same high honor from the universities at Oxford and Edinburgh. He says: "I thought I had four friends in England, but I find I have four thousand."

He wrote in scores of autograph books and albums. He says: "I never refused to write in the birthday book or the album of the humblest schoolgirl or schoolboy, and I could not refuse to set my name, with a verse from one of my poems, in the album of the Princess of Wales, which was sent me for that purpose. It was a nice new book, with only two or three names in it, and those of musical composers,—Rubinstein's, I think, was one of them,—so that I felt honored by the great lady's request. I ought to describe the book, but I only remember that it was quite large and sumptuously elegant, and that I copied into it the last verse of a poem of mine called *The Chambered Nautilus,* as I have often done for plain republican albums."

The press was everywhere most cordial to the famous author. *The London Daily Telegraph* said: "Mr. Lowell and Mr. Holmes are men who combine the culture of the Old World with the indefinable and incommunicable spirit of the New. Both alike are masters of our common language, but each is to the tips of his fingers an American of the Americans."

And why all these attentions to an untitled American,— untitled save in the most royal of all senses—the royalty of brain? Simply because he had given to the world something original, strong, and helpful; in poetry, in science, in fiction, and in essays.

Oliver Wendell Holmes was born in Cambridge, August 29, 1809, the son of Rev. Abiel Holmes, a man of fine intellect and noble character, and of Sarah Wendell, daughter of Hon.

Oliver Wendell. On the father's side, the ancestors served in the old French War and in the War of the Revolution. On the mother's side, the ancestors were among the leading families of New York and New England.

The boy Oliver was a happy, merry child, the third of five children, sensitive, generous, and imaginative. The gentle influences under which he lived were well described by Thomas Wentworth Higginson in 1879: "I should like to speak of that most delightful of sunny old men, the father of Doctor Holmes, whom I knew and loved when I was a child, and hardly knew that there was such a person as Doctor Holmes in the world. The Autocrat once said, and it was an admirable truth, that to have a thorough enjoyment of letters, it was needful that a man should have tumbled about in a library when he was a boy.

"I was brought up in Cambridge, my father's house being next door to that of Doctor Holmes' gambrel-roof house, and the library I most enjoyed tumbling about in was the same in which his infant gambols had first disturbed the repose of the books. I shall always remember a certain winter evening, when we boys were playing before the fire, how the old man, gray and gentle and kindly as any typical old German professor, and never complaining of our loudest gambols,—how, going to the frost-covered window, he sketched with his penknife what seemed a cluster of brambles and a galaxy of glittering stars, and above that he wrote: *'Per aspera ad astra'*—'Through difficulties to the stars.' He explained to us what it meant. I have never forgotten that quiet winter evening and the sweet talk of that old man."

This home of his childhood was especially dear to Oliver. "Ah, me!" he said, years later, "what strains of unwritten verse pulsate through my soul when I open a certain closet in the ancient house where I was born! On its shelves used to lie bundles of sweet marjoram and pennyroyal and lavender and mint and catnip; there apples were stored until their seeds should grow black, which happy period there were sharp little milk teeth always ready to anticipate; there peaches lay in the dark, thinking of the sunshine they had lost, until, like the hearts of the saints that dream of heaven in their sorrow, they grew fragrant as the breath of angels."

When the house was torn down, he said: "With its destruction are obliterated some of the foot-prints of the heroes and martyrs who took the first steps in the long and bloody march which led us through the wilderness to the promised land of independent nationality. I have a right to mourn for it as a part of my life gone from me. . . . I cannot help thinking that we carry our childhood's horizon with us all our days. . . . I am very thankful that the first part of my life was not passed shut in between high walls and treading the unimpressible and unsympathetic pavement."

Oliver's first days at school were under the superintendence of Ma'am Prentiss, who, he says, "ruled the children with a long willow rod which reached across the little school-room, reminding rather than chastising."

"I remember," says the Autocrat, "one particular pailful of water, flavored with the white pine of which the pail was made, and the brown mug, out of which one Edmund, a red-faced and curly-haired boy, was averred to have bitten a fragment in his haste to drink; it being then high summer, and little full-blooded boys feeling very warm and porous in the low-studded school-room where Dame Prentiss, dead and gone, ruled over young children. Thirst belongs to humanity everywhere, in all ages, but that white-pine pail and that brown mug belong to one in particular."

The boy was especially fond of flowers and trees, and when a man did not lose his childish love for them. "When I was of smallest dimensions," he says, "and wont to ride impacted between the knees of fond parental pair, we would sometimes cross the bridge to the next village town and stop opposite a low, brown, gambrel-roofed cottage. Out of it would come one Sally, sister of its swarthy tenant, shady-lipped, sad-voiced, and, bending over her flower-bed, would gather a 'posy,' as she called it, for the little boy. Sally lies in the churchyard, with a slab of blue slate at her head, lichen-crusted and leaning a little now. Cottage, garden-bed, posies, grenadier-like rows of seeding onions—stateliest of vegetables,—all are gone, but the breath of a marigold brings them all back to me."

In the *Autocrat of the Breakfast-Table,* he says: "I love the damask rose best of all. The flowers our mothers and sisters used to love and cherish, those which grow beneath our eaves and by our doorstep, are the ones we always love best. . . . I don't believe any of you happen to have just the same passion for the blue hyacinth which I have,—very certainly not for the crushed lilac-leaf-buds; many of you do not know how sweet they are. You love the smell of the sweet-fern and the bayberry leaves, I don't doubt, but I hardly think that the last bewitches you with young memories as it does me.

"I have a most intense, passionate fondness for trees in general, and have had several romantic attachments to certain trees in particular. . . . I shall speak of trees as we see them, love them, adore them in the fields, where they are alive, holding their green sunshades over our heads, talking to us with their hundred thousand whispering tongues; looking down on us with that sweet meekness which belongs to huge but limited organisms,—which one sees in the brown eyes of oxen, but most in the patient posture, the outstretched arms, and the heavy drooping robes of these vast beings endowed with life, but not with soul,—which outgrow us and outlive us, but stand helpless—poor things!—while Nature dresses and undresses them, like so many full-sized but under-witted children."

The next school of Oliver's boyhood was that kept by William Bigelow, "a man of some wit and a flavor of scholarship." Then for five years he attended a school in Cambridgeport, two of his schoolmates being Margaret Fuller and Richard Henry Dana, author of *Two Years Before the Mast*.

At fifteen, he went to Phillips Academy, where he remained for a year. Here he wrote his first verses, a translation from Book I of the *Æneid*. Fifty years afterward, the lad, now become a famous poet, was asked to read a poem at the centennial celebration of the foundation of the Academy and in this we get a glimpse of that early school-life:

> My cheek was bare of adolescent down
> When first I sought the academic town;
> Slow rolls the coach along the dusty road,
> Big with its filial and parental load;
> The frequent hills, the lonely woods are past,
> The schoolboy's chosen home is reached at last,—
> I see it now, the same unchanging spot,
> The swinging gate, the little garden plot,
> The narrow yard, the rock that made its floor,
> The flat, pale house, the knocker-garnished door,
> The small, trim parlor, neat, decorous, chill,
> The strange new faces, kind, but grave and still:
> Two creased with age,—or what I then called age,—
> Life's volume open at its fiftieth page;
> One, a shy maiden's, pallid, placid, sweet
> As the first snowdrop which the sunbeams greet;
> One, the lost nursling's, slight she was, and fair,
> Her smooth white forehead warmed with auburn hair;
> Last came the virgin Hymen long had spared,
> Whose daily cares the grateful household shared.

· · · · · · · ·

Brave, but with effort, had the schoolboy come
To the cold comfort of a stranger's home.
How like a dagger to my sinking heart
Came the dry summons, "It is time to part."
"Good-by!" "Goo—ood—by!" one fond maternal kiss.
Homesick as death! Was ever pang like this?
Too young as yet with willing feet to stray
From the tame fireside, glad to get away,—
Too old to let my watery grief appear,—
And what so bitter as a swallowed tear!

    .   .   .   .

The morning came; I reached the classic hall;
A clock-face eyed me, staring from the wall;
Beneath its hands a printed line I read:
"Youth is life's seedtime," so the clock-face said.
Some took its counsel, as the sequel showed,—
Sowed—their wild oats,—and reaped as they had sowed.

At sixteen young Holmes entered Harvard College, and was graduated in the class of 1829, which had several members of distinction.

After a year spent in studying law, he decided to become a physician, as more congenial to his tastes. "I never forget the advice of Coleridge," he says, "that a literary man should have a regular calling."

After being under the instruction of Dr. Jackson and his associates for two and one-half years, he spent three years in Europe, chiefly in the hospitals of London and Paris. He also visited the Continent, and came back to his Alma Mater to deliver before the Phi Beta Kappa Society a poem entitled *Poetry; a Metrical Essay*.

Concerning this, James Russell Lowell says, in his "Fable for Critics":

There's *Holmes,* who is matchless among you for wit,
A Leyden jar, always full-charged, from which flit
The electrical tingles of hit after hit.
In long poems 'tis painful sometimes, and invites
A thought of the way the new telegraph writes,
Which pricks down its little sharp sentences spitefully,
As if you got more than you'd title to rightfully.

.   .   .   .

His are just the fine hands, too, to weave you a lyric
Full of fancy, fun, feeling, or spiced with satyric,
In a measure so kindly, you doubt if the toes
That are trodden upon are your own or your foe's.

In the year 1836, when Dr. Holmes was twenty-five years old, his first volume of poems was published. It contained *The Last Leaf,* and that inspiring lyric *Old Ironsides,* written when he was twenty-one, upon the ship *Constitution,* which the government proposed to break in pieces. The poem, published at first in the *Boston Advertiser,* was copied far and near, and the old ship was not destroyed.

The following year his father died, though his mother lived twenty-five years longer, dying at the age of ninety-three. His Boylston prize essays on medical subjects—he gained three prizes—were published in 1838, and won him deserved reputation in the profession. The next year he was appointed Professor of Anatomy and Physiology in Dartmouth College, but resigned two years later, that he might give himself more fully to practice in Boston. He had married in 1840, when he was thirty-one, Amelia, the daughter of Hon. Charles Jackson, formerly judge of the Supreme Court of Massachusetts, and had made his home at No. 8 Montgomery Place, where he resided for eighteen years, and where his three children were born.

Of this place he says, "When he entered that door, two shadows glided over the threshold; five lingered in the doorway when he passed through it for the last time, and one of the shadows was claimed by its owner to be longer than his own. What changes he saw in that quiet place! Death rained through every roof but his; children came into life, grew to maturity, wedded, faded away, threw themselves away; the whole drama of life was played in that stock company's theatre of a dozen houses, one of which was his, and no deep sorrow or severe calamity ever entered his dwelling in that little court where he lived in gay loneliness so long."

During the summer he delivered lectures before the Berkshire Medical School at Pittsfield, Mass., and built a country home there, to which he came for several years.

In 1847, he was made professor in the medical department of Harvard University, which position he honored for thirty-five years. All this time he delivered four lectures each week, besides giving lectures on literary subjects and writing many books. Yet labor never checked the flow of his spirits, nor brought shadows into the sunshine which he made for everybody about him.

His lectures on the "English Poets of the Nineteenth Century" were greatly enjoyed, and especially his fine poems, read after Wordsworth, Moore, Keats, and Shelley. He had the usual experience of lecturers, "Pretty nigh killed himself, goin' about lecturin'; talkin' in cold country lyceums; goin' home to cold parlors, and bein' treated to cold apples and cold water, and then goin' up into a cold bed in a cold chamber, and comin' home next mornin' with a cold in his head."

In 1849, another volume of poems was published, which increased his reputation. Eight years afterward, the *Atlantic Monthly* was started, James Russell Lowell being chosen editor, and Dr. Holmes giving the new magazine its name. Lowell preferred that Holmes should be the editor, for, he said, "Depend upon it, he will be our most effective writer. He will be a new power in letters."

And so it proved. When the *Autocrat at the Breakfast Table* was begun (Dr. Holmes was now forty-nine), its quaint humor, its deep thought, and its freshness and vigor attracted everybody. The *British Review* called it "a very delightful book. A book to possess two copies of; one to be read and marked, thumbed and dog-eared; and one to stand up in its pride of place with the rest on the shelves, all ranged in shining rows, as dear old friends."

How true are the following words. "Don't flatter yourselves that friendship authorizes you to say disagreeable things to your intimates. On the contrary, the nearer you come into relation with a person, the more necessary do tact and courtesy become. Except in cases of necessity, which are rare, leave your friend to learn unpleasant truths from his enemies; they are ready enough to tell them."

"Every person's feelings have a front door and a side door by which they may be entered. The front door is on the street. . . . The side door opens at once into the sacred chambers. . . . Be very careful to whom you give a side-door key. . . . You remember the old story of the tender-hearted man who placed a frozen viper in his bosom, and was stung by it when it became thawed?

"To radiate the heat of the affections into a clod, which absorbs all that is poured into it, but never warms beneath the sunshine of smiles or the pressure of hand or lip,—this is the great martyrdom of sensitive beings."

" 'What do you think, sir,' said the divinity student, 'opens the souls of poets most fully?' . . . Women. Their love first inspires the poet, and their praise is his best reward."

"Our brains are seventy-year clocks. The Angel of Life

winds them up once for all, then closes the case, and gives the key into the hand of the Angel of the Resurrection."

In the *Autocrat* were some of Dr. Holmes's best poems; *The Two Armies,* the *Deacon's Masterpiece,* and *Chambered Nautilus,* which Whittier well says "is booked for immortality":

> This is the ship of pearl, which, poets feign,
>   Sails the unshadowed main,—
>   The venturous bark that flings
> On the sweet summer wind its purpled wings
> In gulfs enchanted, where the Siren sings,
>   And coral reefs lie bare,
> Where the cold sea-maids rise to sun their streaming hair.

The sorrowful days of the Civil War had come, and Dr. Holmes's eldest son, Oliver Wendell Holmes, Jr., had been engaged in it for three years, being wounded at Ball's Bluff, Antietam, and Sharpsburgh. How deeply the father's heart was touched is shown in his article, *My Hunt after the Captain.* His soul was stirred in the cause of freedom, as is shown in *Never or Now* and several other patriotic poems:

> Listen, young heroes! your country is calling!
>   Time strikes the hour for the brave and the true!
> Now, while the foremost are fighting and falling,
>   Fill up the ranks that have opened for you!

Dr. Holmes's next works were *Soundings from the Atlantic,* published in 1864, a collection of prose articles; *The Guardian Angel,* a novel, in 1867; *Mechanism in Thought and Morals,* in 1871; and *The Poet at the Breakfast Table,* in 1872. What an amount of work from one who "lectures so well on anatomy that his students never suspect him to be a poet, and writes verses so well that most people do not suspect him of being an authority among scientific men."

In 1879, when Dr. Holmes had reached his seventieth year,

the publishers of the *Atlantic Monthly* gave a breakfast in his
honor on November 13, chosen as more convenient than the
real anniversary in August. Over one hundred guests assembled at the Brunswick in Boston, W. D. Howells presiding.
After the repast, Dr. Holmes read his poem, *The Iron Gate:*

> I come not here your morning hour to sadden,
>   A limping pilgrim, leaning on his staff,—
> I, who have never deemed it sin to gladden
>   This vale of sorrows with a wholesome laugh.
>
> If word of mine another's gloom has brightened,
>   Through my dumb lips the heaven-sent message came;
> If hand of mine another's task has lightened,
>   It felt the guidance that it dares not claim.

Then followed poems by Whittier, Julia Ward Howe,
Helen Hunt Jackson, Stedman, William Winter, C. P. Cranch,
and Trowbridge, and speeches by Charles Dudley Warner,
President Eliot, J. W. Harper of New York, Aldrich, Higginson, Mark Twain, and James T. Fields.

Mr. Aldrich spoke of Dr. Holmes's "inexhaustible kindness
to his younger brothers in literature. In the midst of a life
singularly crowded with duties, he has always found time to
hold out a hand to the man below him. It is safe to say that
within twenty-five years no fewer than five thousand young
American poets have handsomely availed themselves of Dr.
Holmes's amiability, and sent him copies of their first book.
And I honestly believe that Dr. Holmes has written to each of
these immortals a note full of the keenest appreciation and
the wisest counsel. I have seen a score of such letters from his
busy pen, and—shall I confess it?—I have one in my own
possession!"

For almost ten years after that memorable "Breakfast," Dr.
Holmes worked on, publishing a volume of poems in 1880,

Lives of Motley and of Emerson, his *Mortal Antipathy* in 1886, keeping all the time the kindness and buoyancy of youth, which made him such a delightful companion.

One of his classmates once said of him: "He makes you feel like you were the best fellow in the world, and he was the next best." The charms of his personality were irresistible. Among the poor, among the literary, and among the society notables he was ever the most welcome of guests. His frank, hearty manliness, his readiness to amuse and be amused, his fund of anecdotes, his tact and union of sympathy and originality made him the best of companions.

His wit bubbled up spontaneously, and was all the more appreciated because it came so abruptly and unexpectedly. He was first and foremost a conversationalist. He talked even on paper. Some one has said that, after reading Holmes, we feel that life is easier and simpler and a finer affair altogether and more worth the living, than we had been wont to regard it. Holmes never grew "old"; the winters of four score years and five could not destroy the warm flow of his fellowship and good cheer. "Eighty years young" he was wont to say with one of his genial smiles.

Doctor Holmes was intensely religious. He once wrote to his friend, Rev. Phillips Brooks: "My natural Sunday home is King's Chapel. In that church I have worshipped for half a century. There, on the fifteenth of June, 1840, I was married; there my children were all christened; from that church my dear companion, of so many blessed years, was buried. In her seat I must sit and through its door I hope to be carried to my last resting-place."

Holmes died on October 7, 1894, at the ripe age of eighty-five years, and the world will continue to smile for generations to come because Oliver Wendell Holmes lived. "The wind mourned, the rain fell continuously, as loving hands

bore into King's Chapel, upon Wednesday, October 10, all
that was mortal of the famous poet." The casket, upon which
rested wreaths of pansies and laurels, was borne up the aisle
to the wailing strains of Handel's *Dead March in Saul.* The
funeral sermon was delivered by Doctor Edward Everett Hale,
after which the body of the famous Autocrat was laid to rest
beside his wife in Mt. Auburn.

Harriet Beecher Stowe

THE name of Harriet Beecher Stowe, the illustrious, patriotic author of "Uncle Tom's Cabin," is known in nearly every home in America and in many on the Continent. It is a name closely intertwined with our country's history. "It was the great happiness of Mrs. Stowe," writes George William Curtis, "not only to have written many delightful books, but to have written one book which will always be famous not only as the most vivid picture of an extinct evil system, but as one of the most powerful influences in overthrowing it. . . ."

Harriet Elizabeth Beecher was born in Litchfield, Connecticut, on June 14, 1812. She was the sixth child of Reverend Lyman Beecher, the head of that great family which has left so deep an impress upon the heart and mind of the American people. At the time of her birth he was a poor, struggling Congregational preacher. The mother died when Harriet was but a small child, but she ever retained a loving memory of her.

At the age of five years, Harriet entered the village school.

She was very fond of books and early showed signs of unusual mental ability. When she was eleven years old, she entered the seminary at Hartford, Connecticut, kept by her elder sister, Catherine, and four years later was employed as assistant teacher. About this time her father married again, and brought home a young wife to care for his motherless little ones. Soon after this he accepted a call to the presidency of the Lane Theological Seminary at Cincinnati and moved his family to that place. His daughters, Catherine and Harriet, accompanied them, and founded a new seminary, the Western Female Institute. In 1833, Miss Harriet and one of the associate teachers from the seminary, Miss Dutton, crossed the river and visited in Kentucky. For the first time Miss Beecher was brought into contact with slavery, and the estate where they visited afterward figured as Mr. Shelby's in *Uncle Tom's Cabin*.

Miss Beecher began her literary career in 1834, when her first offering, *A New England Story*, won fifty dollars in a prize competition. Two years later, in her twenty-fourth year, she became the second wife of Calvin E. Stowe, one of the professors in the Lane Seminary, whose first wife had been her intimate friend. They were well suited to each other. "Professor Stowe was a typical man of letters,—a learned, amiable, unpractical philosopher, whose philosophy was like that described by Shakespeare as 'an excellent horse in the stable, but an arrant jade on a journey.' Her practical ability and cheerful, inspiring courage were the unfailing support of her husband."

For a long time after her marriage, money was very scarce in the Stowe home, and Mrs. Stowe wrote stories and articles for newspapers and magazines to help eke out the living expenses. In 1850, Professor Stowe accepted a seat in Bowdoin College and moved his family to Brunswick, Maine. But it was Mrs. Stowe who superintended the packing and shipping of their household effects, transferred herself and the children to the new home, and had everything in readiness and order by the time Mr. Stowe was able to leave Cincinnati. During this trying time, too, Mrs. Stowe still found time to write "more than anybody, or I myself, would have thought . . . for nothing but deadly determination enables me ever to write; it is rowing against wind and tide." That her brave spirit sometimes rebelled against the grind is seen in the following extract from a letter to her husband: "I can earn four hundred dollars a year by writing, but I don't want to feel that I must, and when weary with teaching the children, and tending the baby, and buying provisions, and mending dresses and darning stockings, sit down and write a piece for some paper."

The move to Brunswick, however, showed "the good hand of God visibly guiding the way." With the increased salary and some additional and unlooked-for "luck" in the matter of marketing stories, the Stowes, for the first time in their career, found themselves able to live within their income, and even to lay by a little surplus for a rainy day. The following year, 1851, Mrs. Stowe began the publication of *Uncle Tom's Cabin*, as a serial in the Washington *National Era*. She had contemplated a tale of about a dozen chapters, but once begun the story could be no more controlled than a rudderless ship before the wind, and the serial ran for nearly a year. The story excited intense interest; from all sides came words of praise and encouragement, and eager requests that she keep on with the tale. (It had been announced at first to run only about three months.) This and the growing conviction that she was only the instrument of a Higher Power impelled Mrs. Stowe to finish the work.

She repeatedly said: "I could not control the story, the Lord himself wrote it. I was but an instrument in His hands and to Him should be given all the praise." She indeed wrote as one inspired and could scarcely be induced to leave her work, often rising from her bed at night to pen the words which thronged her brain, dispelling all thought of sleep. She received $300 for the serial rights of the story.

In the meantime, it had attracted the attention of a Boston publisher, who wished to purchase it for publication in book form. He offered Mrs. Stowe a half share in the profits if she would share with him the expense of publication, but the professor objected, saying that they were altogether too poor to undertake such a risk, and it was finally settled that Mr. Jewett should issue the book, paying Mrs. Stowe a ten per cent royalty on all sales. The author waited in trepidation; but her fears lest her book should not be a success were soon dispelled. Three thousand copies sold the first day; the publisher issued the second edition the next week, and the third edition a few days later; in one year over three hundred thousand copies had been issued and sold in this country.

Almost in a day the poor professor's wife became the most talked-of woman in the world, her influence for good spread to the remotest corners; her long struggle with poverty was over; in seeking to aid the oppressed she had aided herself also, and in four months was in receipt of over $10,000 in royalties. Thousands of copies were sold in England, and it was translated into forty foreign tongues, including Arabic and Armenian. It was dramatized and acted in all the leading theaters.

Uncle Tom's Cabin still stands today as one of the most popular novels ever written in America. "It did more than any other literary agency," says Beers, "to rouse the public conscience to a sense of the shame and horror of slavery; more even than Garrison's *Liberator;* more than the indignant poems of Whittier and Lowell or the orations of Sumner and Phillips. It presented the thing concretely and dramatically, and in particular it made the odious Fugitive Slave Law forever impossible to enforce. It was useless for the defenders of slavery to protest that the picture was exaggerated, and that planters like Legree were the exception. The system under which such brutalities could happen, and did sometimes happen, was doomed."

In 1852, Professor Stowe was appointed professor of Sacred Literature in the Andover Theological Seminary, and the family moved to Massachusetts. Mrs. Stowe's health was delicate, and in 1853 in company with her husband and brother, Henry Ward Beecher, she visited England and the continent, where she was everywhere received with universal welcome and made many friends among distinguished people. On returning home, she again took up her pen and for thirty years it was seldom idle. A discerning critic says: "She has entertained and inspired a generation born long after the last slave was made free, and to whom the great question which once convulsed our country is only a name. But her first great work has never been surpassed, and it will never be forgotten."

Harriet Beecher Stowe was a home woman, hospitable and entertaining. She used to say, "Let me once get my feet on the fender and I can talk until the air around me is blue." She was quite absent-minded in her later years. The story is told that she was once invited to visit the daughters of an old friend, and, having been delayed, arrived only a few minutes before dinner was to be served. She was shown at once to her room; the dinner gong sounded, and the family assembled in the dining-room and awaited their guest. Ten, twenty minutes, half an hour elapsed; the bell again sounded but the distinguished guest did not answer the summons, and the now thoroughly alarmed hostesses hurried to her room. There was no answer to their gentle knocking, and they hastily entered. There stood Mrs. Stowe in the center of the room, without even her bonnet strings untied, deeply absorbed in a book. "O, do forgive me, my dears!" she cried contritely, glancing at each alarmed face. "I hope I have not kept you waiting! I found this dear little book here; I have not seen a copy for years, and I couldn't resist looking into it for a moment!"

Mrs. Stowe was a devoted mother. She once wrote to a friend: "Indeed, my dear, I am but a mere drudge, with few ideas beyond babies and housekeeping. As for thoughts, reflections and sentiments, good lack! good lack! yet for all this, my children I would not change for all the ease, leisure and pleasure that I could have without them!"

After the war, the Stowes lived in Hartford in summer, and spent their winters in Florida, where Mrs. Stowe purchased a luxurious home. Mrs. Stowe's mental faculties failed in 1888, two years after the death of her husband; never was she to write again, and she realized it fully, for the enemy had been stealing up by degrees for years, and she had many times been forced into periods of utter rest and relaxation of mind. "My mind wanders like a running brook," she once observed sadly, in one of her lucid moments. "I do not think of my friends as I used to, unless they recall themselves to me by some kind action. . . . I think I am in something of the condition of a silkworm who has spun out all his silk, and can spin no more, unless he has some fresh mulberry leaves. When I reach the 'golden shores,' where grow the trees of life, there I may be able to renew the happy friendships with those who have gone before and may come after me to that happy land."

Harriet Beecher Stowe died at her home in Hartford, July 1, 1896, at the age of eighty-four. By her bedside at the time were her son, Rev. Charles E. Stowe; her two daughters, Eliza and Harriet; her sister, Isabella Beecher Hooker; John Hooker;

Doctor Edward B. Hooker, her nephew and medical attendant, and other relatives. The whole reading world was moved at the news of her death, and many a chord vibrated at the remembrance of her powerful advocacy of the cause of the slave. The good which she achieved by *Uncle Tom's Cabin* can never be estimated, and her noble efforts have been interwoven into the work of the world.

Mrs. Stowe was laid to rest beside her husband and the children who had gone before, in the churchyard at Andover. "Few women have known greater earthly cares," says her biographer. "That she saw her way through them, even while in the valley of darkness, and was able to guide others to the light, giving them the help and support by which she learned to live and to rejoice, proves that this was her mission to the world."

Henry David Thoreau

IME is but the stream I go a-fishing in. I drink at it; but while I drink I see the sandy bottom and detect how shallow it is. Its thin current slides away, but eternity remains. I would drink deeper; fish in the sky, whose bottom is pebbly with stars." So wrote Henry David Thoreau. And again: "Why should we go abroad, even across the way to ask a neighbor's advice? There is a nearer neighbor within us, incessantly telling us how we should behave."

Was there ever more homely and delightful philosophy? And yet it has only been within recent years that the true value of Thoreau's writing has been discovered. His power, however, lies not so much in moralizing, as in his sympathetic idealizing of outdoor life. Reading and study of wild life were the only occupations that satisfied him, and for these he renounced the world. No one ever had greater indifference to fame or less need of public interest than he.

He loved to write: it was the outward expression of his soul. To put on paper, "sentences," as he said, "as durable as a Roman aqueduct"; sentences, which "lie like boulders on the

page, up and down or across—not mere repetition, but crea-
tion, and which a man might sell his ground or cattle to build,"
was with him a thirsting ambition. But he cared little or nothing about getting into print: only two books, *A Week on the
Concord and Merrimac Rivers,*—where he and his brother
roamed in a boat of his own building,—and *Walden,* appeared
during his life-time. He left a great mass of unpublished MSS.
and material scattered about in various "forgotten magazines
and newspapers," which his sister, Miss Sophia Thoreau, and
his friends collected and gave to the world in the *Maine
Woods, A Yankee in Canada, Cape Cod,* etc. Thoreau had the
poet's sensitiveness to every sound and scene of beauty, and
often his feelings found expression in verse.

Henry David Thoreau was born at Concord, Massachusetts,
July 12, 1817, the very year in which Emerson, who was later
to become his dearest lifelong friend, was entering college.
He was the third in a family of four children—two girls and
two boys. "To meet one of the Thoreaus," we are told, "was
not the same as to encounter any other person who might happen to cross your path. Life to them was something more than
a parade of pretensions, a conflict of ambitions, or an incessant
scramble for the common objects of desire. Without wealth,
or power, or social prominence, they still held a rank of their
own, in scrupulous independence, and with qualities that put
condescension out of the question. They could have applied
to themselves, individually, and without hauteur, the motto
of the French chevalier:

> Nor king, nor duke? Your pardon, no;
> I am the master of Thoreau.

As indicated by his name, Thoreau's remote ancestry was
French, but he himself was a thoroughbred Yankee, of the
most ingenious type. He was graduated from Harvard, in 1837,

and, though for a time he was a teacher, as were his brother and sisters, and like them showed no little skill in the profession, he was by no means a scholar in the true acceptance of the term. And, aside from writing, he did not care for scholarly vocations. Indeed, he tells us in *Walden,* "I found that the occupation of paid laborer was the most independent of any," and so, as necessity arose, Thoreau was in turn a skilled surveyor, engineer, carpenter, and on occasion, a gardener, for his farmer neighbors, who respected him not a little, when they found that he knew far more about their fields than they did themselves.

For some time, too, especially in his early years, Thoreau assisted in his father's pencil factory, and indeed carried it on alone for a certain period, until some one could be found to take on this bread-and-butter job of the family. But Thoreau was not a laborer of any sort to any great extent: where was the use? He had no one dependent on him; his wants were few and simple, and for these six weeks of pay sufficed to keep him supplied for a year. The balance of his time, then, he was free to wander where he listed: "to be," as Emerson says, "the bachelor of Thought and Nature."

"O how I laugh when I think of my vague, indefinite riches," wrote Thoreau. "No run on my bank can drain it, for my wealth is not possession but enjoyment." He loved to wander through the fields and woods at all hours, but especially he was prone to start off just about sunset. No writer of modern times has ever produced truer pictures of eventide, night, and early morning scenes, and probably no one was ever more abroad at all sorts of hours than he.

Especially did Thoreau enjoy Nature in her obstinate moods. He loved "to go through a patch of scrub oaks in a beeline, where you tear your clothes and put your eyes out." Drenching rain storms gave "tone to his system," and, indeed, in all the "sours and bitters of nature" his enjoyment was so keen that his readers today cannot help but take part in his enthusiasm. "His essay *Wild Apples*," says one of his admirers, "makes one feel that it would be easy to forego peaches and oranges forever."

No one was ever more at home in the open than Thoreau. Instead of traps or gun, he carried a spyglass, his notebooks and umbrella. Says Emerson, in whose home Thoreau lived for some months as tutor to his boys, and who liked nothing better than to roam afield with the philosopher, or to help him in the orchard and garden: "He knew how to sit immovable, a part of the rock he rested on, until the bird, the reptile, the fish, which had retired from him, should come back and resume its habits,—nay, moved by curiosity, should come to him and watch him." . . . "It was a pleasure and a privilege to walk with him. He knew the country like a fox or bird, and passed through it as freely by paths of his own. . . . He wore straw hat, stout shoes, strong gray trousers, to brave scrub oaks and smilax, and to climb a tree for a hawk's or squirrel's nest. He waded into the pool for the water-plants, and his strong legs were no insignificant part of his armor. . . . Snakes coiled round his leg, the fishes swam into his hand, and he took them out of the water; he pulled the woodchuck out of its hole by the tail, and took the foxes under his protection from the hunters. He confessed that he sometimes felt like a hound or a panther, and, if born among Indians, would have been a fell hunter. But, restrained by his Massachusetts culture, he played out the game in a mild form of botany and ichthyology. His power of observation seemed to indicate additional senses; he saw as with a microscope, heard as with an ear-trumpet, and his memory was a photographic register of all he saw and heard. Every fact lay in order and glory in his mind, a type of the order and beauty of the whole."

All his life Thoreau was a great traveler, but his travels were nearly all in the region of Concord. He never crossed the ocean, nor even saw the Niagara or the Mississippi, until the year before his death. He lived within twenty miles of Boston, but seldom went there, except to pass through it on his way to the Maine woods, or other remote camping grounds. He made few friendships, and cared not at all for the haunts of men, but he was neither churlish nor unsocial. Indeed, he was well-beloved in the home circle, and by all who really knew him.

It was through his friends—Emerson, Daniel Webster, the Brookses, Hoars, and Alcotts, Channing, and good old Dr. Ripley—that Thoreau was persuaded on to the lecture platform, but though his talent here was enjoyed, and the fees, $20 per night, far more than he could earn at manual labor in the same time, he had, as he said, too much "real genius for staying at home" to be often tempted. He would much rather roam the woods for specimens to send to another strong friend —Agassiz—who was thoroughly in sympathy with everything he did in this way. His best-known book, *Walden; or Life in the Woods,* is a record of what he did and saw during the two years he spent in a hermitage, built by his own hands, on the shore of a small lake in Walden woods, about a mile south of Concord. It is a beautiful idyll of sylvan life—the tale of his days and nights with Nature. The site of his cabin is now marked by a cairn of stones gathered from the neighboring field, to which the hundreds of pilgrims who visit it yearly each add a stone.

Though little in sympathy with the common run of men, Thoreau was one of the first to espouse the cause of the slave, and more than one runaway, traveling to Canada and freedom, was lodged in his hut at Walden. He had a high sense of right and wrong, and he went stoically to prison, rather than pay a tax which went to the support of slavery. Emerson, it is said, was horrified at the news, which reached him in a round-about way, and he rushed to his friend at once, demanding: "Henry, *why* are you here?" "Why are you *not* here?" was Thoreau's naïve and honest rejoinder. The following prayer, written by this rigid disciple of Truth, was his guiding precept through life:

> Great God! I ask Thee for no meaner pelf,
> Than that I may not disappoint myself;
> That in my conduct I may soar as high
> As I can now discern with this clear eye.
> That my weak hand may equal my firm faith,
> And my life practice more than my tongue saith;
>
> That my low conduct may not show,
>   Nor my relenting lines,
> That I Thy purpose did not know,
>   Or overrated Thy designs.

Thoreau, impatient of all weaknesses of the physical being, could never learn moderation. He exposed himself in his various pilgrimages to cold, hunger, over-fatigue, and a multitude of hardships, for which he finally paid with his life, having taken a severe cold on one of his camping excursions, which resulted in quick consumption. He died in May, 1862, at the early age of forty-five.

Of Thoreau as a writer James Russell Lowell says: "There are sentences of his as perfect as anything in the language, and thoughts as clearly crystallized; his metaphors and images are always fresh from the soil; he had watched Nature like a detective who is to go upon the stand; as we read him it seems as if all out-of-doors had kept a diary." "He took nature as the mountain-path to an ideal world. If the path wind a good deal, if he record too faithfully every trip over a root, if he botanize somewhat wearisomely, he gives us now and then superb outlooks from some jutting crag, and brings us out at last into an illimitable ether, where the breathing is not difficult for those who have any true touch of the climbing spirit."

Walt Whitman

The youth who reads Poe or Lowell wants to be a scholar, a wit, a poet, a writer; the youth who reads Whitman wants to be a man, and to get at the meaning of real life.—BURROUGHS.

CRITICS of all times have found Walt Whitman almost impossible to define and classify. John Burroughs said of him, "What is he like? He is like everything. He is like the soil which holds the germs of a thousand forms of life; he is like the grass, common, universal, perennial, formless; he is like your own heart, mystical, yearning, rebellious, contradictory, but ever throbbing with life."

Not of domestic or fireside realms is he. Indeed, many of those who know and love poetry do not count Whitman as a poet, and feel that he might as well never have been. His life has been set down as "one of the ironies of literary history." It was his ambition to be the poet of the people—the common mass, the mechanic, the farmer and woodman, fisherman and seaman, the hunter, the bus driver, the soldier, the great world of doers everywhere—for whom, in his endeavors not to seem smug and educated, he discarded every form of style and convention. But the people would have none of him. "We did not think very highly of his writings and found in them more matter for amusement than for instruction," said one of his many friends among these "powerful uneducated persons," as he was wont to term them. *"But we all liked the man."*

"Not a poet of fells and dells," says another, "but of the earth and the orbs. . . . *Vastness* is a word that applies to him. . . . He is a poet plus something else."

Whitman is not to be judged by the law that has so long judged the quality of poets. "I sing myself," said he; hence he is his own law, and we must seek him through the avenues which he himself opens. Measured by old and established modes and formal art, he proves nothing but a disappointment. "A poet's butcher," catalogued Lanier, "one who offers huge raw collops cut from the rump of poetry, and never mind the gristle." "A horrid mountebank, who has given utterance to the soul of a tramp," said another. Adverse criticism, however, hot and heavy though it has always been, does not and cannot dispose of Whitman's own challenge:

Bearded, sunburnt, gray-necked, forbidding, I have arrived,
To be wrestled with as I pass for the solid prizes of the universe.

Emerson early recognized his genius, was, indeed, one of the first to hail him as a bard of promise. His diction, Stedman pointed out, when "on its good behavior, is copious and strong, full of surprises, utilizing the brave, homely words of the people."

When America does what was promised,
When each part is peopled with free people,
When there is no city on earth to lead my city, the city of young
        men, the Mannahatta city—but when the Mannahatta
    leads all the cities of the earth,

When there are plentiful athletic bards, inland and seaboard,
When through these States walk a hundred millions of superb
      persons,
When the rest part away for superb persons, and contribute to
      them,
When fathers, firm, unconstrained, open-eyed—when breeds of the
      most perfect mothers denote America,
Then to me ripeness and conclusion.

Largely we get out of Whitman what we expect to find.
And we may as well give him up in the beginning if we turn
his pages, frowning over his colossal ego in renouncing the old
established form of verse, fuming at his various pieces of au-
dacity, such as that which meets the eye in his apostrophe to
the spotted hawk swooping across his vision,—

    I, too, am not a bit tamed, I, too, am untranslatable,
    I sound my barbaric yawp over the roofs of the world.

Pleasing artistic effects, rounded and finished phrasing are no
part of him; he is a poet, as he is democratic and American, not
by word but by nature. In his own language we have his idea
of what the poet and the poem should be:

    The maker of poems settles justice, reality, immortality,
    His insight and power encircles things and the human race.

Walt Whitman, "the good gray poet," as he has been called,
was born at West Hills, Long Island, May 31, 1819, being the
second of nine children, seven of whom were boys. His father
was a carpenter of English descent, a good workman, but restless and unable to make any headway in the world. His mother
was of Dutch and Welsh descent, and there was, too, some
Quaker blood in her veins. Little Walt, himself, was a sturdy
Dutch baby, with fair skin, hair "black as tar" and blue eyes.
He tells us:

The early lilacs became part of this child,
And grass and white and red morning glories, and white and red
        clover and the song of the phoebe-bird,
And the third-month lambs and the sow's pink-faint litter, and the
        mare's foal and the cow's calf,
And the noisy brood of the barn-yard or by the mire of the pond-
        side.

When the boy was five years old, Lafayette came to Brooklyn, where the Whitman family then resided, to lay the cornerstone of the new public library. As he dismounted from his canary-colored coach, the chubby little Dutch youngster stood square in his path; he picked him up, gave him a hearty kiss and set him in a safe place.

The boy got scanty schooling. He was not much interested in books, and none of his teachers left sufficient impression on him to have even their names remembered. At thirteen he entered a law office as errand boy. His employers were kindly gentlemen, and they undertook to make something out of the lad. He was given a nice desk in a window-nook for his leisure moments, and an attempt was made to improve his hand-writing and to teach him composition. Lastly, and best of all, he was supplied with a card to a big circulating library, and the *Arabian Nights* put into his hands. This was followed by Walter Scott's novels and poetry, and thus the lad was launched on an omnivorous reading career.

While still in his teens young Walt got a job setting type in a printing office, and here, like Franklin and many another young printer, he soon began to think he might write. "The first time I ever wanted to write anything enduring," he said in his old age, "was when I saw a ship under full sail, and had the desire to describe it exactly as it seemed to me." At seventeen he was well known in debating societies in Brooklyn and the surrounding villages. The theater, too, fascinated him.

At eighteen, he turned country schoolmaster and boarded around, having what he later termed "one of the best experiences of his life."

But Whitman had inherited the wanderlust. He could not stick at teaching; there was nothing in farm life that he cared for; and he knew but one other occupation. So he invested in type and presses and set himself up as a country editor. But it must be confessed that he enjoyed best of all his trips on horseback around over the countryside delivering his papers! A year or two sufficed for the youthful editor of *The Long Islander*. Deep within him worked the *motif* he had once outlined for a poem: "Be Happy. Going forth, seeing all the beautiful perfect things." So he drifted away: he could do farm work, if need be, handle carpenter tools on occasion, and set type with the best. Small chance, then, was there of his going hungry, and his other wants were few. In company with his brother Jeff, then fifteen, he tramped through Pennsylvania and Virginia, crossed the Alleghenies, and drifted down the Ohio and the Mississippi to New Orleans. The homeward journey was leisurely pursued by way of Chicago, the Great Lakes, and Niagara. Not until he was well along in the thirties did Whitman show any signs of a settled career. Gradually, however, through the avenue of the composing room and the editorial chair, he drifted into authorship, storytelling being his forte at first.

Whittier's *Songs of Labor* interested Whitman. He, himself, saw dignity in toil, and the very paper which published Whittier's *Shoemaker* had in it a dialogue against Capital Punishment, by Whitman, in which the speakers were The Majesty of the People and A Shivering Convict. "Strangle and Kill in the name of God! O Bible! what follies and monstrous barbarities are defended in *thy* name!" Dickens, too, interested Whitman, and in an article on *Boz and Democracy*, at the time when Dickens was touring America, he said: "I cannot lose the opportunity of saying how much I love and esteem him for what he has taught me through his writings."

"None of Whitman's early prose possesses any high degree of literary merit," says Bliss Perry. "But it is marked by a strong ethical sense and especially by sympathy with the poor and suffering. . . . His stories show a hatred of cruelty and injustice, and a rightmindedness toward the common people, which makes them interesting indications of what was going on in Whitman's mind." His early poems, of a political origin mostly, as were all writings of the day, show no striking qualities, beyond a brisk handling of satire. His first hint of any new rhythmical design, it is claimed, appeared probably about 1852 in a passionate anti-slavery poem *Blood-Money*, with its flaming motto "Guilty of the body and blood of Christ," signed by "Paumanok," a pseudonym Whitman had several times used.

Writing, however, in these early days was only an incident in Walt Whitman's life. He was busy drinking in all manner of sights and sounds; especially did he love to take in Broadway from the top of an omnibus, his favorite position being the seat beside some such skilled handler of the reins as Pop Rice, Broadway Jack, or Balky Bill. All one season he himself drove for "a friend" who was ill, that the man might not lose his place and his family be saved from privation. From his unique vantage point he became familiar with countless of the "powerful uneducated"; he saw, too, all the celebrities of the day, the first ambassadors from Japan, Charles Dickens, the Prince of Wales, Henry Clay, Webster, Andrew Jackson. "He watched James Fenimore Cooper in a courtroom, and called at the *Broadway Journal* office to see its editor, Edgar Allan Poe." His association with newspaper men gave him the free run of all the theaters. He saw and knew personally many

of "the kings and queens of the footlights." He reveled in the
Italian opera as delivered by Alboni, Grisi, and Mario. Often
as he rode up and down the Bowery he shouted stormy passages from *Julius Caesar* into the "dense and uninterrupted
street-bass." Sometimes for a week or two at a stretch, he would
slip away to the country or seashore, taking with him the Bible,
Shakespeare, Ossian, or some translation from Homer, Aeschylus, Sophocles, the old German Nibelungen, and special ver-
sions of ancient Hindu poems.

But Whitman was not in any sense a student of literature.
"I feel about literature," he is reported to have said, "as Grant
did about war. He hated war. I hate literature. I am not a
literary West Pointer; I do not love a literary man as a literary
man." . . . "I don't care much for Milton or Dante." Goethe
he hardly knew. He "couldn't swallow Hugo's exaggeration
and bombast." And, speaking of Dr. Johnson, he didn't admire
"the old man's ponderous arrogance. . . . He lacks veracity."
Scott and Tennyson he liked; Browning was "not for me";
Stevenson reduced him to oaths; Swinburne was "the damn-
dest simulacrum"; Cooper roused him to enthusiasm; Thoreau was "an egotist"; Lowell struck him with indifference, he
felt that "he is not likely to be eternally useful." In short,
Whitman had a slighting opinion of most of his literary contemporaries. He knew little of the life that comes through
books, deliberately rejecting it and the housebound life of what
people called "society."

Houses and rooms are full of perfumes, the shelves are crowded
          with perfumes,
I breathe the fragrance myself and know it and like it,
The distillation would intoxicate me also, but I shall not let it.

His own poetical style, embodied in his *Leaves of Grass,* was
undoubtedly formed largely from the Old Testament bards,

and the Hindu and Persian poets, *I* (who am present every-where in divers forms) being especially pronounced in the latter works. He tells us, in *Song of Myself,*

> I celebrate myself, and sing myself
> And what I assume you shall assume,
> For every atom belonging to me as good belongs to you.

No haughty individualist, proud of his singularity, he is,

Walt Whitman, a kosmos, of Manhattan the son,
Turbulent, fleshy, sensual, eating, drinking and breeding,
No sentimentalist, no stander above men and women or apart from
     them.

Telling us that

> I find no sweeter fat than sticks to my own bones,

he insists that

In all people I see myself, none more and not one a barley-corn less,
And the good and bad I say of myself I say of them.

The "I" whom he celebrates is far more than a simple personal pronoun. And he says,

> You will hardly know who I am or what I mean,
> But I shall be good health to you nevertheless,
> And filter and fibre your blood.

> Failing to fetch me at first keep encouraged,
> Missing me one place search another,
> I stop somewhere waiting for you.

Whitman heartily despised riches and all worldly success; any outward show and finery were to him mere hollow shams. He went about habitually clad in gray—wide-brimmed slouch hat, rough flannel shirt, open at the neck. "The common

people—workingmen, the poor, the illiterate, the outcast—
saw themselves in him." He would not have accepted the finest
home as a gift on condition that he live in it. When his brother
Jeff contemplated building a house, he advised him to forego
architects and construct a mere shanty—a place to eat and
sleep were all-sufficient.

Few men were so deeply stirred by the Civil War as was
Whitman. It aroused in him a vast fund of sympathy and patriotism, and in 1862, when his brother Lieutenant-Colonel
George Whitman, 51st New York Volunteers, was wounded
at Fredericksburg, he left at once for the scene of action to do
what he could as an army nurse, the while he supported himself and provided many necessities for "his boys" by sending
home letters to Northern newspapers. Of the great service he
rendered to the wounded and homesick soldiers we can speak
but briefly. "He did the things for them no nurse or doctor
could do, and he seemed to leave a benediction at every cot as
he passed along." His letters to his mother, published under
the title *The Wound Dresser,* and *Drum Taps,* now included
in *Leaves of Grass,* give vivid pictures of camp and hospital
experiences—pictures that show not the brilliancy of victory
and military prowess but the sorrow and anguish that follow
the train of war, "night's darkness and blood-dripping wounds,
and psalms of the dead,"—and in these passages are some of
Whitman's finest work. Read *Come Up from the Fields,
Father,* and the two Lincoln memorial poems *My Captain,* and
When Lilacs Last in the Door Yard Bloom'd. The latter poem
has been called "The noblest elegy in the language." And its
hymn to death, beginning,

> Come lovely and soothing death,
> Undulate round the world, serenely arriving, arriving,
> In the day, in the night, to all, to each,
> Sooner or later delicate death,

Swinburne called "The most sonorous anthem ever chanted in the church of the world."

It was just after the war, while Whitman was still keeping up his visits to the wounded in Washington hospitals, that John Burroughs, a clerk in the government department, chanced upon the "good gray poet" in the woods, one Sunday afternoon, and then and there was begun the warm friendship which ended only with Whitman's life. Shortly, Whitman, too, had a clerkship in the Indian department, and in this connection we must not forget an interesting anecdote: In company with certain officials, Whitman made a trip to Kansas to see some Indians who were in the custody of the law. Carefully the sheriff told off the distinguished names of the investigators, but the Indians paid them small heed, all but turned their backs, in fact. At the end of the procession came Whitman, alone and unannounced. The old chief roused instantly; one quick searching look he gave to the Manhattanese, and then he extended his hand. "How!" he said, cordially, and all the other Indians at once followed suit. Nothing, perhaps, could have given Whitman greater pleasure. It is said that Lincoln, who did not know Whitman personally, once peeped at him from a window in the Congressional halls. "Well," he exclaimed, "he looks like a *Man!*"

The last days of the poet's life were spent at Camden, New Jersey, in a small frame house, rather unsightly and weather-beaten, on an unlovely street, but Whitman was indifferent to the ugliness and discomfort. A housekeeper, "whose passion for sewing lace collars on the poet's shirts exceeded her zeal for the broom and dustpan, a black cat, a spotted dog, a parrot, and a canary, completed the household. . . . Here he was visited by hundreds of persons eager to look upon his very noble face and to touch the hand which he used to extend with a royal graciousness. Sometimes they were asked to partake of one of his simple meals. Some of them brought little gifts: fruit, or his favorite mixture of coffee, or a bottle of wine. He loved to share these delicacies with the sick and poor of the neighborhood. Painters painted his portrait; sculptors made busts; photographers, knowing that Heaven might never send them another such a subject, photographed him until, as Whitman himself remarked, "the very cameras were weary."

Many of Whitman's callers came from over the sea. Occasionally the caller might be "a tramp, an anarchist, a socialist, a Japanese art-student, an enthusiastic college girl." Newspaper men kept the trail well-worn. In 1885, when the poet became too lame and infirm to get about the streets, a subscription, limiting the donors to $10 each, was circulated to purchase a horse and buggy, and the sum was quickly secured. Thereafter, his friends frequently contrived little donations for him. "What we want most in the world," wrote Mark Twain, "is to keep the old soul comfortable." In 1886, on the occasion of his Lincoln lecture, which he had been giving annually for a number of years, and which he continued until the last year of his life, his friends gathered in a body, and quietly swelled the admissions to nearly $700. In 1887, Andrew Carnegie paid $350 for his seat. The end came March 20, 1891, following an onslaught of pneumonia. Imagine the surprise of his zealous friends to learn as Whitman lay dying, that he whom they had supposed to be penniless had built for himself a massive $4000 tomb in Harleigh Cemetery, and had several thousand dollars in the bank!

The year after Whitman's death there was brought out, in New York, an elaborate and complete edition of his work, comprising ten volumes. And today the American public, with Whitman no longer before them in person to irritate by his "striking *poseur* attitudes," find in him veins of native ore, and he is daily becoming better understood and enjoyed. *Leaves of Grass* has been translated, in whole or in part, into many languages, and Whitman is known all over the world.

Samuel L. Clemens (Mark Twain)

MARK TWAIN (as Samuel L. Clemens will always be known) did not live or write simply to amuse the world. He always saw the ludicrous, which he exposed with an unerring instinct, but he also saw the true, the pure, the genuine in mankind. He was a close student of human nature with a heart as warm as his perceptions were keen.

He was thoroughly American, and loved and believed in his own country. At the close of *A Tramp Abroad* he says: "I was glad to get home—immeasurably glad; so glad, in fact, that it did not seem possible that anything could ever get me out of the country again. I had not enjoyed a pleasure abroad which seemed to me to compare with the pleasure I felt in seeing New York harbor again. Europe has many advantages which we have not, but they do not compensate for a good many still more valuable ones which exist nowhere but in our own country." Yet he has not failed to depict the snobbery of some of our people who, after spending eight weeks in Paris, address their friends with a French accent. "It is not pleasant," he says, "to see an American thrusting his nationality forward *obtrusively* in a foreign land; but, oh, it is pitiable to see him making of himself a thing that is neither male nor female, neither fish, flesh, nor fowl—a poor, miserable, hermaphrodite Frenchman!"

Samuel L. Clemens was born in Florida, Monroe County, Missouri, November 30, 1835. The family soon moved to Hannibal, in the same State, where the fun-loving boy, not fond of study, but active in mind and body, lived the life so graphically portrayed in *The Adventures of Tom Sawyer*. When requested by his mother to whitewash a fence, with consummate management he made his friends believe that the work was a pleasure, and actually hired out the labor to them, receiving in return for his generosity "twelve marbles, part of a jew's-harp, a piece of blue-bottle glass to look through, a spool cannon, a key that wouldn't unlock anything, a fragment of chalk, a glass stopper of a decanter, a tin soldier, a couple of tadpoles, six fire-crackers, a kitten with only one eye, a brass door-knob, a dog-collar—but no dog—the handle of a knife, four pieces of orange peel, and a dilapidated old window-sash." Meantime he sat upon the fence and ate apples, while they worked.

When taken to Sunday School—not usually going of his own free will, because he loved blue skies and sunshine better—he managed to obtain enough tickets to procure a Bible as a prize. However, when questioned by the visitor who happened to be present, as to the names of the twelve apostles, with some gentle coaxing he gave the names of two as "David and Goliah!"

The delightful boy-and-girl love of Tom Sawyer and Becky Thatcher is inimitably told, and runs like a golden thread through all that young life, pathetic in its poverty and fresh and natural in its enthusiasm. Only a noble and tender heart could have taken the blame upon itself when Becky accidentally tore the teacher's book, and received "without an outcry the most merciless flogging that even Mr. Dobbins had ever administered," and "when he stepped forward to go to his punishment the surprise, the gratitude, the adoration that shone upon him out of poor Becky's eyes seemed pay enough for a hundred floggings."

When young Clemens was twelve years old, his father died, leaving the household without means, as he had lost all by endorsing notes for friends. He was one of a fine Virginia family, several of whom had been in Congress, and he also was a man of brain and force of character. The mother was a warm-hearted woman, kind to every living creature, with great emotional depths, and unusual felicity in her choice of words, either in speaking or writing. Left with four children, they must needs do their part in the struggle for support. Samuel went to school ostensibly, where, he says, he "excelled only in spelling," but loved to spend much of his time upon the river, and so successful was he in getting into its turbid waters that he was dragged out of it nine times before he was fifteen. Evidently it was not his fate to die by drowning.

In these early years he tried various methods of earning a livelihood, and finally learned printing, in the office of the *Hannibal Courier,* of which he says, in his book of *Sketches,* that it had "five hundred subscribers, and they paid in cord-wood, cabbages, and unmarketable turnips." With a desire to see himself in print, his first articles appeared during a week's absence of the editor. So personal were they that the town was stirred, and the paper was in jeopardy. However, it resulted in thirty-three new subscribers, all of whom wished to read what was written about their neighbors, and the journal "had the vegetables to show for it, cordwood, cabbage, beans, and unsalable turnips enough to run the family for two years!"

After he had been nearly three years on the paper, he made

up his mind to run away and see the Exposition in New York. He had been earning fifty cents a week, and had saved the necessary funds. Arriving in New York, he had twelve dollars in his pocket, a ten-dollar bill of which sum he had sewed into his coat sleeve. When the Exposition had been duly examined, he found work in John A. Green's printing office, but after two or three months he met a man from his town, Hannibal, and, fearing that his whereabouts would be reported, he suddenly took his departure for Philadelphia, working on the *Ledger* and elsewhere. While here, when taking the part of a poor boy who was imposed upon by a fireman, he was severely beaten by the latter, so that "he resembled Lisbon after the earthquake," he says. Finally he made up his mind that he had experienced enough of the Eastern world, and, with his ten dollars still sewed into his coat sleeve, went back to his Missouri home.

All these years he and his boy friends had cherished, as he says in *Old Times on the Mississippi,* an ambition to be steamboat-men. "We had transient ambitions of other sorts, but they were only transient. When a circus came and went, it left us all burning to become clowns; the first Negro minstrel show that came to our section left us all suffering to try that kind of life; now and then we had a hope that if we lived and were good, God would permit us to be pirates. These ambitions faded out, each in its turn, but the ambition to be a steamboat-man always remained. . . . I first wanted to be a cabin boy, so that I could come out with a white apron on and shake a tablecloth over the side, where all my old comrades could see me; later I thought I would rather be the deck hand who stood on the end of the stage plank with the coil of rope in his hand, because he was particularly conspicuous. But these were only daydreams—they were too heavenly to be contemplated as real possibilities. . . . By and by I ran away. I said

I never would come home again till I was a pilot and could come in glory. But somehow I could not manage it. I went meekly aboard a few of the boats that lay packed together like sardines at the long St. Louis wharf, and very humbly inquired for the pilots, but got only a cold shoulder and short words from mates and clerks. But I was ashamed to go home. . . . I was in Cincinnati, and I set to work to map out a new career. I had been reading about the recent explorations of the River Amazon by an expedition sent out by our government. It was said that the expedition, owing to difficulties, had not thoroughly explored a part of the country lying about the head-waters, some four thousand miles from the mouth of the river. It was only about fifteen hundred miles from Cincinnati to New Orleans, where I could doubtless get a ship. I had thirty dollars left; I would go and complete the exploration of the Amazon. I packed my valise, and took passage on an ancient tub, called the *Paul Jones* for New Orleans. For the sum of sixteen dollars I had the scarred and tarnished splendors of 'her' main saloon principally to myself, for she was not a creature to attract the eye of wiser travellers. When we presently got under way and went poking down the broad Ohio, I became a new being, and the subject of my own admiration. I was a traveller. A word never had tasted so good in my mouth before. . . . I kept my hat off all the time, and stayed where the wind and the sun could strike me, because I wanted to get the bronzed and weather-beaten look of an old traveller. Before the second day was half gone, I experienced a joy which filled me with the purest gratitude; for I saw that the skin had begun to blister and peel off my face and neck. I wished that the boys and girls at home could see me now."

After two weeks the *Paul Jones* reached New Orleans, and the young traveler soon discovered two things. "One was that a vessel would not be likely to sail for the mouth of the Amazon

under ten or twelve years; and the other was that the nine or
ten dollars still left in my pocket would not suffice for so im-
posing an exploration as I had planned, even if I could afford
to wait for a ship. Therefore it followed that I must contrive
a new career. The *Paul Jones* was now bound for St. Louis.
I planned a siege against my pilot, and at the end of three hard
days he surrendered. He agreed to teach me the Mississippi
River from New Orleans to St. Louis for five hundred dollars
payable out of the first wages I should receive after graduating.
I entered upon the small enterprise of 'learning' twelve or
thirteen hundred miles of the great Mississippi River with the
easy confidence of my time of life. If I had really known what
I was about to require of my faculties, I should not have had
the courage to begin."

The work proved hard and discouraging for the youth, but
he finally reached the desired position of pilot, and had the
proud satisfaction of receiving two hundred and fifty dollars
per month. Here he remained for five years, till he was twenty-
six, when the growth of railroads and the Civil War made
piloting unprofitable.

For a few weeks he served in the Confederate Army, but
soon went with his brother, who had been appointed Lieu-
tenant-Governor of Nevada Territory, as his private secretary.
The details of this exciting trip overland have been read by
thousands in that fascinating book, *Roughing It*. The work of
the secretary proved to be nothing and with no salary, so that
he spent considerable time in fishing in Lake Tahoe, "but we
did not average one fish a week." Then for amusement he
purchased an animal of Mexican breed, and his description
of riding upon him, when he was "shot straight into the air
a matter of three or four feet," or clasped the neck of the creature, who "delivered a vicious kick at the sky, and stood on his
forefeet," is unsurpassed in the annals of horseback experi-

ence. "Everybody I lent him to always walked back; they never could get enough exercise any other way."

Clemens finally decided to try his hand in silver mining. He had always considered himself lucky. He had passed through cholera, yellow fever, and smallpox epidemics, had seen thousands die around him, but he had come out unscathed. "I never expected things, and never borrowed trouble," he says. A wise philosophy, to be learned early in life if one would succeed. Why should he not be lucky also in mining? The great silver-mines in Nevada were being opened. A poverty-stricken Mexican traded a stream of water for one hundred feet of a mine, and four years later was worth a million and a half. Teamsters became millionaires. The whole territory was wild with excitement. "I would have been more or less than human if I had not gone mad like the rest," says Mr. Clemens. "Cart-loads of solid silver bricks as large as pigs of lead were arriving from the mills every day, and such sights as that gave substance to the wild talk around me. I succumbed and grew as frenzied as the craziest." He and a few friends moved from Carson two hundred miles to the mines. "We built a small, rude cabin in the side of the crevice and roofed it with canvas, leaving a corner open to serve as a chimney through which the cattle used to tumble, occasionally, at night, and mash our furniture and interrupt our sleep. . . . We went to work; we decided to sink a shaft. So for a week we climbed the mountain, laden with picks, drills, gads, crowbars, shovels, cans of blasting powder and coils of fuse, and strove with might and main. . . . We prospected and took up new claims, put 'notices' on them, and gave them grandiloquent names. . . . We had not less than thirty thousand feet apiece in the 'richest mines on earth,' as the frenzied cant phrased it—and were in debt to the butcher. We were stark mad with excitement—drunk with happiness—smothered un-

der mountains of prospective wealth—arrogantly compassion-
ate toward the plodding millions who knew not our marvellous cañon—but our credit was not good at the grocer's. . . .
We were always hunting up new claims and doing a little work
on them, and then waiting for a buyer, who never came. . . .
At last when flour reached a dollar a pound, and money could
not be borrowed on the best security at less than *eight per
cent a month* (I being without the security, too), I abandoned
mining and went to milling. That is to say, I went to work as
a common laborer in a quartz mill, at ten dollars a week and
board." The work was so hard that Clemens remained only
one week, and then asked an advance of wages.

"He said he was paying me ten dollars a week, and thought
it a good round sum. How much did I want?

"I said about four hundred thousand dollars a month, and
board, was about all I could reasonably ask, considering the
hard times. I was ordered off the premises! And yet, when I
look back to those days and call to mind the exceeding hard-
ness of the labor I performed in that mill, I only regret that
I did not ask him seven hundred thousand."

At last Clemens and his friend Higbie found their mine.
By the laws of the district, claimants must do a reasonable
amount of work on the ledge within ten days from the date
of location. Clemens went away to care for a sick friend, supposing Higbie would attend to their fortune. Unfortunately,
the latter went to other work, supposing that another person
would do the necessary labor. Both men returned ten days
later to find that other parties had secured their claim, and
held millions of dollars in their hands, while Clemens was as
poor as ever. He certainly had not been lucky in mining. He
was "blue" indeed; not sky-blue, he says, but indigo. Possibly
if he could have looked forward to the future and seen himself
living in a comfortable home, and famous the world over, the
skies would have looked more golden.

About this time an offer came from the Virginia City *Enterprise,* for which paper he had already written some articles, signing himself here, for the first time, "Mark Twain," taken from the speech of the leadsmen on the Mississippi River, in making soundings. The paper offered him twenty-five dollars a week as city editor. He was indeed thankful. He would gladly have taken three dollars a week.

"Twenty-five dollars a week—it looked like bloated luxury—a fortune, a sinful and lavish waste of money. But my transports cooled when I thought of my inexperience and consequent unfitness for the position, and straightway on top of this my long array of failures rose up before me. . . . Necessity is the mother of 'taking chances.' I do not doubt that if at that time I had been offered a salary to translate the Talmud from the original Hebrew, I would have accepted, albeit with diffidence and some misgivings, and thrown as much variety into it as I could for the money."

For two years he held this position, and then, desiring a change, moved to San Francisco. For a time all went well, but soon the large amount of mining stocks in his trunk proved worthless. Writing for the newspapers, and receiving a small amount of money, irregularly, is not conducive to peace of mind or health of body. The struggles of these days, as given in *Roughing It,* are, alas, too true. For a time he was on the staff of the *Morning Call,* and then went to the Sandwich Islands (now the Hawaiian Islands) to study the sugar business and write letters for the *Sacramento Union.* He showed much journalistic enterprise, and his work was greatly enjoyed by all who read it.

On his return, the old question of self-support presented itself. What should he do next? He decided to give a lecture. He had never stood before an audience. His friends, with one exception, enthusiastically said "no" to his suggestion. But he hired the new Opera House at half price, and on credit, for sufficient reasons. "In three days I did a hundred and fifty dollars worth of printing and advertising, and was the most distressed and frightened creature on the Pacific coast. I could not sleep—who could, under such circumstances? For other people there was facetiousness in the last line of my posters, but to me it was plaintive with a pang when I wrote it: 'Doors open at 7½. The trouble will begin at 8.' "

To Mr. Clemens' amazement the house was packed, and he cleared six hundred dollars. Then he dared to try New York. He judiciously gave free tickets to all the public schools, and was delighted to find that Cooper Union was full. Evidently, the skies were growing brighter. Courage and persistence had won their way.

In 1867, when Mr. Clemens was thirty-two, he joined a pleasure party going abroad in the "Quaker City." The party visited France, Italy, and Palestine. On their return, the humorist wrote *The Innocents Abroad, or The New Pilgrim's Progress,* and it was sold by subscription. The book was eagerly purchased and read from one side of America to the other, and in Europe as well. In Europe, a German Count was urged by a young lady to read *The New Pilgrim's Progress,* from its delightful humor, as she had just finished it. He purchased the book at once, but failed to find the fun she had told him of. Upon showing her the book, she saw that he had purchased *Pilgrim's Progress* by Bunyan!

Whether we read how Mr. Clemens bought gloves too small for him at Gibraltar, because a young lady flattered him, and threw them away the next morning, or lingered tenderly by the bust of Christopher Columbus, or described mountain and city with vividness and beauty, we were amused, delighted, and instructed. "Mark Twain" had become famous, and poverty had become a thing of the past.

In 1870, Mr. Clemens was married to Olivia Langdon,

whose brother he had known on the "Quaker City." She was beautiful, as well as pleasant; and now luck had come indeed. Her father, a man of large wealth, purchased a home for them in Buffalo, and Mr. Clemens bought a third interest in the Buffalo *Express*.

Fortunately, Mr. Clemens did not remain in journalism, else probably we should have missed his books. *Roughing It* appeared in 1871; *The Gilded Age,* written jointly with Charles Dudley Warner, in 1873; "Beriah Sellers' Infallible Imperial Oriental Optic Liniment and Salvation for Sore Eyes—the Medical Wonder of the Age"—with headquarters for manufacturing in Constantinople, and hindquarters in Farther India! "Annual income—well, God only knows how many millions and millions apiece!" Who can ever forget the candle in the stove, giving the appearance of heat, and the unique supper of "Early Malcolm turnips, that can't be produced except in just one orchard, and the supply never is up to the demand." As pathetic as all this is humorous is the death of Squire Hawkins, leaving wife and children destitute, still hoping for the rise of Tennessee land.

In 1876 *Tom Sawyer* that classic of boyhood was published, "affectionately dedicated to my wife"; in 1880, *A Tramp Abroad*.

After this, in 1882, appeared *The Prince and the Pauper,* dedicated "to those good-mannered and agreeable children, Susie and Clara Clemens," two of his four daughters. It is the tender story of a Prince and Pauper changing places, the hardships of one and the joy of the other, the breaking-down of Tom Canty when he sees his mother in the crowd, and the restoration of the rightful prince. We grow kinder at heart as we read the book, and see that circumstances often make or unmake us, and we learn charity and sweetness in the study of human nature.

Then came *Huckleberry Finn* based on a boy character who first appeared in *Tom Sawyer*. As Huck tells it in the opening chapter of the book, "You don't know about me without you have read a book by the name of *The Adventures of Tom Sawyer,* but that ain't no matter. That book was made by Mr. Mark Twain and he told the truth, mainly." In *Huckleberry Finn,* the question of truth is as irrelevant as it is in *Tom Sawyer.* If the raftsmen whom Huck meets on his trip down the river didn't behave as they do in the book, they certainly should have. And if those delightful scalawags, the Dauphin and the Duke of Bilgewater, were not drawn from life, life was poorer without them.

Besides his work as an author, Mr. Clemens, was also an inventor on a small scale. His scrapbooks sold over one hundred thousand yearly. "As he wanted a scrapbook, and could not find what he wanted, he made one himself, which naturally proved to be just what other people wanted." Similarly, he invented a notebook. It was his habit to record, at the moment they occurred to him, such scenes and ideas as he wished to preserve. All notebooks that he could buy had the vicious habit of opening at the wrong place and distracting attention in that way. So, by a single contrivance, he arranged one that always opened at the right place; that is, of course, "at the page last written upon."

Mr. Clemens established the publishing house of C. L. Webster in New York City, in 1884. The following year they published the *Memoirs of U. S. Grant,* the profits of which, amounting to $350,000, were paid to Mrs. Grant in accordance with their agreement. This company failed eleven years later, and Mr. Clemens found himself a poor man and morally though not legally, responsible for large sums due to creditors. He resolved to wipe out every dollar of the debt, and at once entered upon a lecturing trip around the world, meeting with personal welcome and such financial success as his motive merited.

Later books from his pen included: *A Yankee at the Court of King Arthur* (1889); *Puddinhead Wilson* (1894); *Tom Sawyer Abroad* (1894); *Joan of Arc,* which was published anonymously in 1896, and created a literary sensation until its authorship was established; *A Double-Barreled Detective Story* (1902); and various articles on Christian Science in which he spoke out in his usual straightforward fashion. An *Autobiography* which appeared serially also attracted wide attention. Its fascinating pages revealed that Mark Twain knew everybody that was worth knowing.

Mark Twain indeed became one of the most famous men on earth, in his old age. Says a press reporter: "He was not merely a man; he was an institution. He was a sort of neighborhood settlement of good cheer, with many branches located in the oases as in the waste places, where admission and refreshment were free to all. Millions—how many millions is beyond estimating—came and partook of his wine of optimism and stayed for supper. Though an American born, he belonged to all lands. He had traveled in all lands, and lived in most of them. He had more near-permanent homes perhaps than any other man of his day. Nearly always he was a wanderer, sometimes from necessity, more frequently from choice."

And right here comes in an interesting little anecdote that is too good to miss: One evening Brander Matthews and Francis Wilson were dining together, when the former proposed that they write to Mark Twain.

"But," objected Mr. Wilson, "we don't know where he is."

"Oh," said Professor Matthews, "that doesn't make any difference. A letter will reach him all right."

Accordingly the two wrote the letter, and addressed it: "Mark Twain, God Knows Where."

In due time they received a telegram from Mr. Clemens which said briefly: "He did."

Mark Twain, though styled the "King of Humor," was often quite serious. He was one of the closest observers of human nature and institutions, places and things, that ever lived. Even in his most humorous books we find that he has made accurate transcripts of the things which impressed him. Though he exaggerated, a privilege belonging to his profession, one can read between the lines the inhering truth. He was an inveterate foe to shams of every sort, and apparently knew his highest happiness when with droll sarcasm he punctured a popular fraud with his pen.

Master of the empire of laughter and also of tears, Mark Twain's own life yet lacked much of being a primrose path. We have seen how he encountered stumbling places and had steep hills of difficulty to climb in his public career, but nothing has been said of his many private "sorrows that bit and griefs that bludgeoned." Some of these griefs found their way into his later works. Books like *What Is Man?* and *The Mysterious Stranger* are full of what Bernard De Veto has called "the symbols of despair," and they reflect the tragic and the bitter in man's life. At the close of his life, April 21, 1910, so far as relatives were concerned, he was almost alone in the world, being survived only by his daughter, Clara, who had married a foreigner and resided abroad.

Mark Twain's surest title to fame generally is believed to be *Tom Sawyer* and its companion volume, *Huckleberry Finn,* both of which Theodore Roosevelt carried with him through Africa, and read many times. The works of the great optimist have been translated into many languages. "Printer, pilot, reporter, humorist, novelist, philosopher—he is safely embalmed to enduring fame."

Louisa May Alcott

O N a summer's day more than a hundred years ago, the steamer from Philadelphia was ploughing its methodical way toward Boston. There was nothing very remarkable about the voyage—in fact most of the passengers considered it a dull trip. But there was one little girl who was having the time of her life. Down in the engine room they found her, intently watching the marvelous machinery. She was entirely unconscious of everything else . . . even of the fact that her best nankeen frock was covered with grease and dirt.

This was two-year-old Louisa May Alcott.

With her sister Anna and her parents she was going back to New England. At least it was "back to New England" for the family, even if the two children had been born in Pennsylvania. Several years before, her father, who was teaching school in Boston, had been persuaded by a rich Quaker gentleman to pull up stakes and move to Germantown. There he would educate this man's seven children and whatever other pupils there might be. But Bronson Alcott had as usual been entirely too optimistic. Pupils were scarce, and after the sponsor's death the Alcotts had to come away.

Yet it must have been a relief to the two elder Alcotts now to come back to the city which they knew so well. They quickly settled down and Masonic Temple School, as it was called, was reopened. Alcott was a good teacher. His students liked him. And his personality attracted people. His income grew to a hundred and fifty dollars a month—quite a sum in those days. The Alcotts, comparatively speaking, were living amid prosperity!

Considering that Louisa's father was such a well-known schoolmaster, it seems rather strange that she herself never attended his classes. In fact, as she explained, she really did not go to any school at all. But this hardly meant that there was no studying to do. Her education began at the age of three! Each morning there were lessons in the library. Louisa May Alcott hated grammar. She did not like arithmetic either. But how she did love the reading hour, when they went through *Pilgrim's Progress,* and Krummacher's *Parables*—books which nowadays may not sound quite so exciting.

Little Louisa had always lived quite in the midst of books. One of her earliest memories, she said, was of the times when she played in her father's study, building houses and bridges with Bacon and Plutarch. Often she pretended to be writing something very important, and left her scribbling all over the blank pages of the somber volumes.

However, she did not stay in the house all of the time, probably, at this stage, very little of the time. She said herself that as a child she was very much of a tomboy—ran races, climbed trees, and was always on the go. One afternoon, at the age of six, she drove her hoop all the way around the Boston Common without stopping, a feat which was viewed with the greatest admiration by her friends.

And one of her choicest diversions was running away, for Louisa was a child with insatiable curiosity and a great desire for exploration on a small scale. There is a story about the time, when a very little girl, she spent part of one day playing with several children among some fascinating ash-heaps. They shared with her their lunch of fish, cold potatoes and crusts. After lunch Louisa left her new-found friends, and set off to make a tour of the Common. When it was a question of going home, she did not know exactly where home was, and curling up next to a big shaggy dog on a front door step, she went sound to sleep. The town crier, sent by her frantic parents, came by ringing his bell and shouting out her description. "Why, dat's me," she exclaimed as she woke up. The crier fed her a most wonderful supper of bread and molasses and returned her to the family.

Louisa was growing up like any city girl and things were going very well with the Alcotts in Boston. Suddenly something happened which spoiled everything. A visiting English author, who spent less than an hour in Bronson Alcott's classroom, published a harsh criticism of his teaching methods. At the same time one of his own books happened to offend the religious feelings of some of the Boston people. The fat was in the fire! Pupils left one after another. The school failed and the schoolmaster Alcott realized that the best thing for him to do was to move somewhere else.

Now one of Bronson's friends was none other than Ralph Waldo Emerson, and Emerson suggested that he come out to Concord to live. The family moved at once, and took up their residence in a little cottage surrounded by a garden. It cost only $50 a year.

Louisa's father had imagined that he could make a living by working in the country and giving occasional lectures. He was sadly disappointed. Woodcutter or lecturer, he made very little, and the family, which now contained four daughters, was not faring well at all. Emerson, the loyal friend, did everything he could to get employment for Mr. Alcott, but it was no use. Alcott himself was discouraged and he finally became so melancholy and despondent that Emerson gave him five hundred dollars and sent him off to Europe. (In those days a trip to Europe was expected to do wonders for almost any ailment of body or mind.)

Now Mr. Alcott was an idealistic, if impractical person, and he was constantly trying to organize life on a higher social plane. Like Emerson, he was a transcendentalist, believing in the spiritual life, as contrasted with the material life. He was a staunch vegetarian, and even in Boston the family had had to live on a diet of boiled rice and graham meal. There were people in England who were inspired by his theories and charmed by his engaging personality. It is not altogether strange that three of these converts returned with him— Charles Lane with his son, William, and Henry Wright.

They had great plans for a socialist colony, a sort of Massachusetts Utopia. The three guests settled down at the Alcott's home, Hosmer Cottage, during that winter and throughout the long evenings they made their schemes and dreamed their dreams for the New Eden. When spring came, a farm was purchased. They gave it the name of "Fruitlands," and moved in.

Emerson himself was frankly sceptical of the whole thing, and, as it turned out, the experiment was most disastrous. No adequate provision had been made for winter. The members departed one by one, and finally "Fruitlands," with its fine-sounding name, was entirely deserted.

As an event in history this dramatic failure is not important, but what is important is the fact that one of America's future writers was taking it all in, absorbing part of this experience every day. How different her education was from what we think of when we say "education" today. It is such a natural thing to attend regular classes in a public school and to go from the Sixth Grade to the Seventh, and so on. Everyone remembers what teachers he had and the friends he knew in any certain grade of school, but none of those things were part of Louisa May Alcott's life. The Alcott children had had instead the close companionship of their father, and he always delighted in working with them. Often he would lie full length on the floor, drawing letters and making diagrams. He taught them much about writing and gave them lists of words to spell. He always insisted too that his children were prodigies, and when they lived in Boston showed them off so much that they became very much talked about.

Mrs. Alcott, too, had much to do in the education of her daughters, particularly in the education of Louisa. She herself did not sympathize with all of her husband's ideas. In fact she was not at all enthusiastic about the New Eden plan. Sensibly, Mrs. Alcott said little about it. But she gave the child encouragement.

The children were obliged to keep diaries, in which they wrote down their thoughts, and these were inspected periodically by the parents. Louisa began hers at the age of seven! Hardly more than a baby, she noted down her thoughts and aspirations. Also all her struggles with her conscience . . . which in Louisa's case began very early in life.

It was the custom of her mother to write little notes to the girl, and on her tenth birthday there was a pencil-case, with a note saying that her mother had seen how fond she was of writing, and this was a habit to be encouraged. Perhaps, in fact, that was something that had been noticed two years before, for at the age of eight Louisa had written a poem about a robin and her mother reading it proudly exclaimed, "You will grow up a Shakespeare!"

While her mother gave her the encouragement, Mr. Lane, who now was the children's teacher, gave her the practice. He drilled her constantly in writing and in conversation, on subjects which seem to us difficult, to say the least. For the day's composition he would ask her to write a conversation between Themistocles, Aristides and Pericles. They would discourse on moral precepts. First he would ask her what virtues she would wish more of, and after Louisa enumerated them, he would ask what vices she wished less of. Sometimes Mr. Lane would take the part of Socrates, twelve-year-old Louisa the part of Alcibiades, and they would converse on matters of morals and ethics, using Platonic dialogue.

As a matter of fact Louisa did not like Mr. Lane very much, but this kind of discipline certainly must have stood her in good stead later when she came to write. It seems as though she had almost too much discipline. In her journals (at ten years of age) she tells how she got up each day at five and had her bath. Adding that she *loved* cold water! Before breakfast there would be the singing lesson with Mr. Lane, and after breakfast she washed the dishes. The morning would be given over to lessons. There would be a dinner of bread and fruit and during the afternoon the children would read, walk or play. At ten years of age she read Martin Luther, Mrs. Child's *Philothea* and at fifteen Bettine's correspondence with Goethe. Often she would talk with her father and his friends on the question of the abolition of slavery, Man's place in the world, and other profound matters.

It is a relief, however, to read that this child, so surrounded by ideas and intellectual activity, had her normal outdoor life too. In fact she always regarded the Concord days as the happiest of her life. There were many companions, for the Emersons and the Hawthornes were her playmates. An inseparable companion there was named "Cy." Cy induced her to chew the tobacco that the farm hands gave her and Cy, one day, persuaded her to rub her eyes (much to her regret) with red peppers. Out in the barn they reenacted their fairy tales in glorious fashion—Cinderella and Jack-the-Giant-Killer. They pretended some days they were fairies, and held their revels among the trees, and together they lived in that delightful world of "pretend." It is a relief to know that she vaulted fences like a boy, and that she loved to run through the woods when the dew was still on the grass. It is reassuring to know that she played with dolls, and stole the rooster's feathers in order to make doll bonnets. It was not entirely transcendentalism after all.

In spite of her remarkable ability Louisa May Alcott did not achieve literary success without a struggle. After the Alcotts moved into Boston again from the country, there were years, desperate years of hard work. Her mother set about earning money for the family's support. First she was a relief worker and finally took in boarders. Louisa did nearly everything. She taught. She did needlework. She even became a domestic servant at two dollars a week. But always her fingers itched for the pen, and when Sunday came at last, she wrote down the plots and stories which had been teeming in her mind the other six days.

Finally the time came when she sold her first story. Louisa made very little of it, hastily pointing out that the story had been written in Concord when she was but sixteen. Nevertheless it was important, for now she was writing to sell. Papers like the *Gleason's Pictorial Drawing-Room Companion* and Boston *Saturday Evening Gazette* bought stories from her regularly, paying the princely sum of five dollars each.

Then the time came when her manuscripts were accepted by the *Atlantic Monthly*. But Louisa did not dare to go to the offices herself and talk with the editor, the great James Russell Lowell. Her father had to deliver the material for her. Her crowning success came, as we all know, when Louisa May Alcott produced *Little Women*.

She had already written one novel called *Moods,* which was far from successful. It had been forgotten in several months. But for ten years she had had the idea of writing the account of her own extraordinary family. It would be called *The Pathetic Family*. Now the *publishers* made a request for a girl's story. She started to write it, but the work went very slowly. Miss Alcott declared she didn't like the job much, and let the winter go by without getting very far. When spring came, she sat down, and with a sudden burst of energy wrote the whole first part in six weeks. During the fall she put in another mad six weeks of intensive work and finished the second part. When completed, it was indeed the story of "the pathetic family": May, Jo, Beth and Amy were none other than Louisa and her three sisters.

Perhaps it was because she knew them all so well and saw them so vividly that the book was such an unprecedented success. People loved it, and overnight it became the rage of 1869. They stopped each other on the street to ask, "Have you read *Little Women?*"

At last Louisa May Alcott had achieved the fame she deserved so well, and in that year of 1869 she was scarcely less famous throughout the country than the great Emerson, who had patted her head when she was a little girl.

Edith Wharton

FASHIONABLE New York in the 1860's and 1870's was a town of horses and carriages, houses with brownstone fronts, formal dinners, and fastidious manners. It was into this society that Edith Newbold Jones was born on January 24, 1862. Her ancestors were well-known New York shipping merchants of English heritage with a sprinkling of Dutch and French. Her father was not a businessman—he was a "gentleman who never spoke about money." Very few of the Joneses' friends or relations were engaged in a business or profession. Because of the enormous increase in value of New York real estate most of the old families lived on fortunes made from selling portions of their lands. Mrs. Jones was a fine hostess and a beautifully dressed woman. Edith admired her mother's lovely clothes, and once when an aunt asked her what she would like to be when she grew up she replied, "The best dressed woman in New York." Born into this fashionable world, cultivated yet not intellectual, it is odd that Edith Wharton should become not the best dressed woman in New York but one of the best loved authors in the United States.

Edith's earliest memories were of the hours she spent playing on the sunny lawns of Roman villas, rolling hoops and skipping rope, or driving through the old romantic streets with her governess. Then there was a carriage journey to Spain over little-traveled roads and through orange groves and fields of olive trees. It was in Paris the following winter that Edith began her storytelling. With a shaggy copy of Washington Irving's *Alhambra* in her hands—as often as not upside down —the little girl would walk up and down in her room making up stories about "grownups." The book seemed to be a necessary prop, and she would turn the pages at the proper intervals as though she were really reading. Edith had playmates, but she preferred to be alone with her imaginary people. Sometimes when a "nice little girl" was brought over to spend the afternoon Edith would run to her mother and beg, "Mamma, you must go and entertain that little girl for me. I've got to make up."

Edith never spent long hours in a schoolroom. A series of governesses and tutors taught her Italian, French, and German when she was hardly more than a baby, and to these languages were added other studies suitable for a young lady in those days. Because she had had a serious case of typhoid fever when she was very small her parents felt that she should not "strain" her mind, and Greek and Latin were omitted from her curriculum. She never had to concentrate on subjects which were not interesting to her, and the modern languages, good manners, and a careful use of the English language were her chief lessons.

After six years of wandering in Italy, France, Spain, and Germany the Joneses returned to New York—to the winter season of opera and balls and to the fashionable summers in Newport, Rhode Island. In contrast to the great cathedrals, spacious palaces, and historic streets of Europe, New York

seemed small and ugly, but it was here that Edith discovered
the delights of her father's library. Now she had a chance to
read to her heart's content and, peeping into all the books hidden behind the glass doors of the bookshelves, she made her
acquaintance with many classics. Her mother refused to allow
her to read novels, so that although she missed some great
stories by good authors, her mind was not cluttered with the
light novels of the day. There were classics in French, German,
and English; many poets; some historians; a few philosophers;
some books of travel. With this fury of reading grew an increased desire to "make up" and this time to write it down.
No one took the girl's scribbling seriously, nor was any paper
provided for her scratchings. When packages came to the
house she would snatch the wrapping paper and carefully fold
it and add it to the store in her room. If the urge came for her
to write she would spread the big sheets on the floor, and her
pencil would fly as she wrote the stories about her imaginary
people.

When Edith was seventeen she made her debut and began
the social round of lunches and dinners, operas and after-thea-
ter suppers, afternoon calls and formal balls. In Newport in the
summer she played tennis in a long dress and a sailor hat, enjoyed boating trips, or in the afternoon dressed in her most
elaborate costume with a veil and a sunshade drove along the
Ocean Drive or made a round of polite calls. She was a thought-
ful-looking girl with big dark eyes and brown hair which she
wore in a bang, probably half to follow fashion and half to hide
a high and prominent forehead which made her look more intellectual than the other debutantes. When she was twenty she
married Edward Wharton, a "gentleman of leisure" from Boston. He was some fifteen years older than she, but an earlier
romance had come to nothing when the young lawyer whom
she loved had been called away from New York. Wharton was

a "good match" and his persuasiveness overcame her uncertainty. They moved into a cottage on her family's estate at Newport where for several years they lived from June till February. Every February they sailed for Europe for four months of travel. They spent much time in Italy, and one year they hired a yacht with some friends and enjoyed a glorious cruise in the Mediterranean.

The remodeling of the cottage in Newport was responsible for Edith Wharton's first book. She had already written a few poems, which had been accepted by *Scribner's, Harper's,* and *Century.* Now with an architect friend she redecorated the inside of her house, and the description of their work and the principles involved form the text of *The Decoration of Houses* which was published in 1897. Then Mrs. Wharton began to write stories for magazines, and in 1899 her first volume of short stories was published, *The Greater Inclination.* When this little volume became a success she realized that writing was to be her chosen work. This decision had a curious effect on her family and New York friends. That particular circle had never produced an author, and Edith Wharton's growing success seemed to embarrass them. None of her old New York friends or relations ever mentioned her books when they talked with her. It was as though she had never written them, and her literary life and acquaintances were completely apart from the life and friends she had known before. She made many lasting friendships in the literary world among whom were Henry James, the great short story writer and novelist; Clyde Fitch, the dramatist.

Shortly after the publication of *The Greater Inclination* the Whartons sold their Newport house and built a large home in Lenox, Massachusetts. This was real country; there were gardens in which Mrs. Wharton loved to work, and beautiful meadows and woods. There was a lake nearby and all the quiet delights of the country were hers. They spent six or seven months a year at this place which they named "The Mount." Some days they took long drives through the hills and little villages of western Massachusetts. They talked with the people who lived in the back country and saw the quiet lives they and their ancestors had led for generations. Here she continued her writing, publishing more short stories and short novels. In 1902 came *The Valley of Decision* which grew from her Italian trips and was a tale of eighteenth-century Italy. Because of her knowledge of Italian architecture she was commissioned to write a book on Italian buildings of the seventeenth and eighteenth centuries, and the result was *Italian Villas,* which has for years served as a text for students of architecture. This was followed by *Italian Backgrounds,* which describes some of the impressions of her extensive travels in Italy.

Just as her wanderings in Italy showed results in her writing, so did her long summers and winters at Lenox. *Ethan Frome* and *Summer* are novels about the cramped existence in the tiny villages of western Massachusetts. *Ethan Frome* is considered by many people to be her best novel. A smaller book than her others, and one which does not show the influence of Henry James, it is her acknowledged masterpiece, and her own favorite. Deeply tragic, it presents a convincing picture of the narrow bitter village lives, the poverty and loneliness of the villagers.

But Edith Wharton is perhaps best known to most readers as the writer of society stories. Born and brought up as she was in fashionable New York society she turned her thoughts back naturally to this life of her girlhood and wrote of the circle that she knew so well. As a little girl "making up" she had always imagined her stories about grownups like her handsome father and beautifully dressed mother, their activities and their friends. Now she took the old New York scene, and on this scene her imaginary characters came to life.

The House of Mirth was the first of these society novels. It tells of the frivolous world of New York, the men struggling to keep enough money ahead to pay for the extravagant tastes of their wives, the gossip, the clothes, the flirtations, the scandals.

The Age of Innocence shows the great importance to the New Yorker of this period of keeping to the proper pattern and doing what was "correct," and what happened when one tried to be independent. This novel placed Mrs. Wharton with the top-ranking American writers. Although she never particularly wanted to be a "best-selling" author the popularity of *The Age of Innocence* gave her this distinction. It also won her the Pulitzer prize.

All this time she continued her travels. In addition to the continent she visited in England, and met many entertaining literary people. After 1907 the Whartons spent each winter in Paris. Here, as on her travels, she tended her husband, whose mental health began to show signs of serious disturbance. Eventually, his sanity became completely impaired, but she cared for him still. Even though the beau of her youth, now a successful international lawyer, had come into her life once more, she remained with her husband. Finally, however, he had to be given over to the care of a specially trained attendant, and in 1912, owing to his condition, they were divorced. Even then Edith Wharton refused to resume the romance that had been interrupted in her early years. She never married again, though Walter Berry, the man in question, remained her devoted friend and literary adviser.

At the outbreak of the first World War Mrs. Wharton was in Paris. All during the struggle she gave her time and money to relief. There were many French women and children without jobs, and she organized and directed a workshop for seamstresses, collecting money from Americans in Paris to finance the work. Later she formed committees and raised large sums for refugees and relief. There were "Edith Wharton" committees in New York, Washington, Boston, and Philadelphia raising funds and working ceaselessly. The devoted service which she gave to the Allied cause made her an internationally known figure. Her work took her all along the rear of the fighting-line trenches. In her book, *Fighting France,* she described the conditions that she found. *The Marne,* a short story, and *French Ways and Their Meaning* helped to make the French people more understandable to the Americans. *A Son at the Front* is a study of the war world behind the front. During the twenties Mrs. Wharton's novels deteriorated in quality.

After the war Mrs. Wharton moved to a quiet house surrounded by big trees and gardens in the suburbs not far from Paris where, with her gardening and writing and occasional travels, she led the life that she always preferred. It was there on August 11, 1937, that she died.

Edith Wharton was an indefatigable writer. In forty years she wrote forty-five books. Her subjects were widely different —from *The Writing of Fiction* to her books about Italy, from the simple, narrow, country background of *Ethan Frome* to the elaborate New York society of *The Age of Innocence* and *The House of Mirth.* Several of her books were dramatized, and the great success of *Ethan Frome* and *The Old Maid* on the stage and in the moving pictures is well known. Her last book, *The Buccaneers,* was not finished at her death, but the outline was complete, and the book was published in 1938, a splendid example of her skill in characterization.

Whether she wrote of drawing rooms or battlefields, Italian villas or country towns, Edith Wharton pictured flesh and blood people in real situations. She wrote of things about which she knew, about the society into which she was born, and lands through which she had traveled. Often she laughed at her characters; sometimes she treated them with deep sympathy; always she is a master of style, characterization and plot.

Willa Cather

P RESENTLY," says a character in one of Willa Cather's finest books, "we saw a curious thing: There were no clouds, the sun was going down in a limpid, gold-washed sky. Just as the lower edge of the red disc rested on the high fields against the horizon, a great black figure suddenly appeared on the face of the sun. We sprang to our feet, straining our eyes toward it. In a moment we realized what it was. On some upland farm, a plough had been left standing in the field. The sun was sinking just behind it. Magnified across the distance by the horizontal light, it stood out against the sun, was exactly contained within the circle of the disc; the handles, the tongue, the share—black against the molten red. There it was, heroic in size, a picture writing on the sun."

The passage might well be taken as representative of Willa Cather's life work. Her novels and stories are concerned with simple but important things like the earth, the sun, the sky, and the ordinary, humble people who work upon it and beneath them. But just as the slanting rays of the setting sun seem to enlarge objects in their path, so Miss Cather makes things that we often overlook appear significant. She does this not by pointing her finger and shouting, "This is important!" Instead, she merely pictures a scene or a person for us. She focuses our attention just as the disc of the sun does. In doing so, she uses no distortion. She does not omit certain things in order to stress others. We see all the details, just as we see "the handles, the tongue, the share" of the plough. As a result her pictures seem as natural as those objects seen against the evening sky. They are "heroic in size," but they are, none the less, true to life, real.

Despite the fact that Miss Cather refuses to point or shout, her pictures are replete with meaning. Seeing the plough standing in the field at evening, we are made aware, in some mysterious fashion, of the dignity of labor. We seem to hear echoes of the Biblical injunction about gaining a living through the sweat of the brow. Life can be simple without being superficial. And it is so in Miss Cather's books. For, like Ántonia, a character in one of her novels, Willa Cather drew on "a rich mine of life." And she is able to stop one's breath for a moment, as Ántonia did by a look or gesture "that somehow revealed the meaning in common things."

The rich mine of life began for Willa Cather on December 7, 1873, on the family farm at Willowshade in the hills of Back Creek, Frederick County, Virginia. Her parents were of the generation that had grown up during the Civil War, a generation she describes in her last book as "gayer and more carefree then their forbears, perhaps because they had fewer traditions to live up to. The war had done away with many of the old distinctions. The young couples were poor and extravagant and jolly. They were much given to picnics and camp-meetings in summer, sleighing parties and dancing parties in the winter." It was in just such an atmosphere that young Willa, or "Willie" as she preferred to be called, spent the first ten years of her life, helped by an indulgent mother to generous portions of the rich stream of experience that Southern hospitality caused to flow through the house. Indeed, it was Willa's mother who provided her with the opportunity to witness the reunion of an old Negress and her daughter who, as a beautiful young girl, had run away from slavery twenty-five years before. The episode, described almost sixty years later in the epilogue to *Sapphira and the Slave Girl,* was to provide her with the plot for her last novel.

It was during these early years, too, that young Willa ac quired her sympathetic understanding of nature. Virginia in the spring, when the oak leaves are "no bigger than a squirrel's ear" and the "mountain stream rushed coffee brown, throwing up crystal rainbows where it gurgled over rock ledges," made a lasting impression on her young mind. She was particularly delighted, as anyone who has ever spent a spring in Virginia must be, when "from out the naked grey wood the dogwood thrust its crooked forks starred with white blossoms—the flowers set in their own wild way along the rampant zigzag branches . . . the wildest thing and yet the most austere, the most unearthly."

Happily, Willa Cather retained the impressions of Virginia that she had gathered so precociously. For in her tenth year her father sold Willowshade and took his family—Willa had two younger brothers and a sister by this time—to the far different country of the Great Divide, in sparsely settled Nebraska. Describing winter in that country, she says, in *O Pioneers!,* her first distinguished book: "The variegated fields are all one colour now; the pastures, the stubble, the roads, the sky are the same leaden gray. The hedgerows and trees are scarcely perceptible against the bare earth, whose slaty hue they have taken on. The ground is frozen so hard that it bruises the foot to walk in the roads or in the ploughed fields. It is like an iron country, and the spirit is oppressed by its rigour and melancholy. One could easily believe that in that dead landscape the germs of life and fruitfulness were extinct forever." To the little mountain girl the great, undulating prairies seemed "nothing but land: not a country at all, but the material out of which countries are made." And she had the feeling that "the world was left behind."

The world had been left behind—the world of her childhood. But to a girl with such sharp perceptions as Willa Cather had there was beauty even in the untamed West. There would be no more Virginia springs with their delightful signs. But there was "—spring itself; the throb of it, the light restlessness, the vital essence of it everywhere; in the sky, in the swift clouds, in the pale sunshine, and in the warm high wind—rising suddenly, sinking suddenly, impulsive and playful like a big puppy that pawed you and then lay down to be petted." In its more savage moods, however, nature in this new land was far from puppyish. Not many people of fine sensibility could stand up to it. In Mr. Shimerda of *My Ántonia* Willa Cather reveals the tragic capitulation of one such individual, driven to suicide by the isolating loneliness of a Nebraskan blizzard.

Miss Cather was made of sterner stuff. She could watch the awful beauty of an electric storm with thunder "loud and metallic, like the rattle of sheet iron" and lightning breaking "in great zigzags across the heavens." And she could recall the scene later in her books—"Half the sky . . . checkered with . . . thunderheads, but all the west . . . luminous and clear: in the lightning-flashes it looked like deep blue water, with the sheen of moonlight on it; and the mottled part of the sky was like marble pavement, like the quay of some splendid sea-coast city, doomed to destruction."

She could not then, when the cornfields were widely separated by wild prairie, foresee that they would "enlarge and multiply until they would be . . . the world's cornfields . . . one of the great economic facts . . . which underlie all the activities of men, in war or peace." But she could make the empty prairies significant by remembering tales like those which told of Coronado's northward march from Mexico into the Midwest, or that which told of the sunflower trail laid down by the Mormon leaders scattering seed as they journeyed westward, seeking a new home for the persecuted believers who followed in the spring. For Miss Cather the sunflower-bordered roads of the Midwest would ever after be "the roads to freedom."

Along these roads came the Bohemians, Austrians, Germans, French, Russian, Danes, Norwegians, Swedes, all of the immigrants from the Old World who, following in the wake of the pioneers, brought their rich old languages and full cultures to the empty new land. Young Willa Cather's curiosity led her to seek out these people, and she often rode miles on horseback, delivering mail as a pretext for entering some of the lonely scattered sod farmhouses where she could meet them and learn something of their customs and of the lands from which they had come. It was in these houses that she met people like Mr. Shimerda, who didn't take even children for granted, and Neighbour Rosicky, who had spent his youth in three lands and who was interested in something more than merely "getting on." He knew that "you could not enjoy your life and put it in the bank too."

After a little over a year on the farm on the Great Divide, Willa Cather's family moved into the nearby town of Red Cloud, where her father went into business. Here Willa and the rest of the children—two more brothers and another sister swelled the crowded Nebraska household—delighted in the long unfinished attic in which they all slept in the little house just a block from the main street of the small western town.

Here, too, Willa began her formal schooling. She was lucky enough to find instructors like her music teacher. He realized that she had little interest in learning to sing or play an instrument. But he saw that she responded to music and liked to talk about it. Wisely, he spent his time with her playing the great music that he knew or talking about the men who made it. She was even more fortunate in finding, in the small town, friendly, cultured people like the Wieners, who encouraged her to study French and German and to make use of the large collection of books in both of those languages which their library contained.

It was in Red Cloud that Willa Cather met "Uncle Billy" Drucker, a self-taught merchant who could usually be found leaning over the counter of his store deep in a copy of the classical poets. Supplementing her adequate but limited curriculum, she began to read Latin and Greek with "Uncle Billy." His passionate devotion to classical poetry was contagious, and it sustained the young scholar when, in later summers, she returned from the dry-as-dust lectures at the university in Lincoln. One of her earliest and deepest sorrows was the death of this beloved teacher. She found him one summer lying dead on his couch, his copy of the *Iliad* open beside him.

"Uncle Billy" was laid to rest in the windswept graveyard outside of Red Cloud. Among the conventional tombstones in that cemetery was one that stirred the imagination of the young authoress-to-be. It was the massive, rugged red boulder that marked the grave of Silas Garber, a Nebraskan pioneer who had founded one of the first communities in the area and who later became Governor of the state. During his lifetime Willa had known Silas Garber and had often visited him and his charming wife in their large house just south of Red Cloud. Here she had met the trail breakers, the founders of

cities, the railroad builders, "the dreamers, great-hearted ad-
venturers" who had settled the Old West. Later she put them
all, including Silas Garber (as Captain Forrester) and his
strange monument, into a novel called *A Lost Lady*, a novel
about "the visions those men had seen in the air and followed,"
putting "plains and mountains under an iron harness."

Not all of the inhabitants of Red Cloud were like "Uncle
Billy" or Silas Garber, however. The town had its share of
mean, petty, unlikeable people. There were those townsmen
of Anglo-Saxon stock who considered themselves "native
Americans" and who objected to their immigrant neighbors
because they were "not our own kind." Culturally limited and
ignorant of the rich background of these immigrants, the
"native Americans" rejected the vigor and the rich variety of
the ways of their neighbors, taking refuge in an empty "refinement." It was such people who emptied life of its meaning.
Often shrewd and unscrupulous in business because they
lacked an understanding of the significance of life, they were
people like Ivy Peters in *A Lost Lady*, "who never dared anything, never risked anything. They would drink up the mirage,
dispel the morning freshness, root out the great brooding spirit
of freedom, the generous easy life of the great land-holders.
The space, the colour, the princely carelessness of the pioneer
they would destroy and cut up into profitable bits. . . ." It
is because the philosophy of these people has come to dominate the West that *A Lost Lady* is the picture of "the end of
an era, the sunset of the pioneer."

The respectable and the refined did as much as they could
in Red Cloud, as they do everywhere, to make life joyless and
pallid and dull. But the snobbish appeal to associate with
"the people we know" had no meaning for Willa Cather. "It
was just my point," she says, "that I saw altogether too much
of the people we knew." She got to know others. She met the

hired girls whom the respectable found so objectionable. They were Bohemian and Scandinavian girls who came to town to work, helping to clear the family homesteads in the surrounding district from debt, and they were objectionable primarily because "their beauty shone out too boldly against a conventional background." Among them Willa Cather got to know many of the beautiful girls whom she was to describe in her books, girls like friendly Ántonia, bold Bohemian Mary, and langorous, violet-eyed Lina Lingard.

Furthermore, although the town was a small one made dull by refinement, it offered plenty of variety to the sharp-eyed young Willa. Observing her fellow townspeople, she quickened her powers of perception. And from her store of early observations she is later able to draw people of all types: people like Mrs. Cutter, whose face "was the very color and shape of anger," and the disconsolate telegrapher at the depot, who saved pictures of actresses that he got with cigarette coupons and "almost smoked himself to death to possess those desired forms and faces." Perhaps someone like blind D'Arnault, the Negro pianist, with his "shrunken, papery eyelids," came to play in Red Cloud during Willa Cather's youth. And Larry Donovan, the passenger conductor, must have stopped there often between trains. This latter personage is characterized as "one of those train-crew aristocrats who are always afraid that someone may ask them to put up a window, and who, if requested to perform such a menial service, silently point to the button that calls the porter. Larry," Miss Cather concludes with telling insight, "wore this air of official aloofness even on the street, where there were no car-windows to compromise his dignity."

At the age of seventeen Willa Cather left Red Cloud for Lincoln and the University of Nebraska. Here she studied languages and literature with great diligence, but she could not understand mathematics and only succeeded in overcoming her deficiency in freshman mathematics just before she graduated. If the quality of instruction in the university was not as inspiring as she might have hoped, she refreshed herself during her summer vacations, reading Latin and Greek with "Uncle Billy." She found an outlet for her imagination, too, in writing for and editing the *Hesperian,* an undergraduate literary publication. The friendships she made among Lincoln families were an added source of pleasure. And in the family of the chancellor of the university, James H. Canfield, she found not only intellectual stimulation, but a lifelong friendship with the girl who was to be, as Dorothy Canfield Fisher, a famous novelist herself.

The years which Willa Cather spent at the university were hard years for Nebraskans. Several successive crop failures gave rise to a general depression which reduced Willa's father, among others, to desperate financial straits. Fortunately, Willa was able to help out. She had taken a course in journalism with Will Owen Jones, the managing editor of the *State Journal,* who for a time gave special instruction at the university. Jones liked Miss Cather's work and invited her to become a regular contributor to his paper at a dollar a column. She was soon producing a sufficient number of columns to maintain her at the university until she received her degree in 1895. Furthermore, her articles were excellent enough to attract the attention of Charles Axtell, a Pittsburgh businessman who was founding a new magazine. Shortly after her graduation, Axtell invited Miss Cather to come East as an editor of the Pittsburgh *Home Monthly.* The invitation was accepted, and Miss Cather left Red Cloud for Pittsburgh and a career in journalism in the summer of 1896.

Pittsburgh opened new vistas for the young Westerner. It was not only the "legends of the iron kings" and the flaming

evidence of the steel mills—"the very incandescence of human energy"—that excited her. The museums and art gal-
leries, the libraries and concert halls provided by the new
wealth of the smoky city attracted her even more. The theater
became a passion with her, and when she got to know some
of the performers she thought of the stage door as "the actual
portal of romance." Her job was less satisfactory, for she was
expected to provide "entertainment for the idle hour . . .
pure and clean in tone" to "more than half a million firesides"
in the area surrounding Pittsburgh. Overworked—she was
managing editor in all but name and salary—, understaffed,
and hedged about by puritanical restrictions, she left the
Home Monthly after her first year for a job with the *Daily
Leader,* Pennsylvania's largest evening paper at the time.
Here, despite a certain amount of drudgery, she was happier,
particularly when she commenced writing dramatic criticism
for the paper. But even here she had little time for the creative
fiction which she wished to devote herself to. Consequently,
she turned to teaching. From 1901 to 1906 she taught English
and Latin in Pennsylvania high schools. Though she now had
more time for the short stories that she contributed to periodicals with increasing frequency, she took her job as a teacher
seriously and felt in later life that she had succeeded better at
teaching than in anything she had undertaken before she became a writer.

To her teaching years belong also her first books, *April Twi-
lights,* a volume of verse, and *The Troll Garden,* a book of
short stories. Both of these books were written, after years of
drab, comfortless boarding house existence, in the settled and
comparatively luxurious environment of wealthy Judge Mc-
Clung's home. Soon after she began to teach, Willa had met
Isabelle, the judge's young daughter. The two became fast
friends and spent a summer abroad together—an important

experience for Willa. Upon their return Isabelle invited Willa
to come and live in the large McClung home. Here, in the
small study provided by her friend's generosity, the two books
were written. They were important only in that they were a
start. They proved to the young author that with leisure and
peace of mind she could become a serious artist. But she was
not to have the leisure for a long time yet. For the short stories
came to the attention of S. S. McClure, New York publisher
of *McClure's Magazine,* and he went to Pittsburgh to see their
author and take her back to serve on the editorial board of his
magazine. He was a forceful man and his magazine had a
national reputation. Moreover, Willa, remembering the plight
her father had been in while she was at college, could not resist
the desire for security, a security which a position with Mc-
Clure insured. She accepted his offer and came to New York
late in 1906.

She was to stay with the magazine for six years, becoming
managing editor and boosting the circulation by sixty thousand during her first year of responsibility. The job was not
an easy one. Besides turning out stories and articles, she directed the policy of a magazine that became infamous among
conservatives for its exposés of villainy and stupidity in national life and politics. It was to the type of journalism epi-
tomized in *McClure's* that the epithet "muckrakers" was applied—applied in angry derision, but worn proudly as a badge
of integrity by the contributors. However, despite her involve-
ment in this stirring journalistic activity, Miss Cather managed to produce her first novel, *Alexander's Bridge,* while
working for the magazine. She also revisited Europe. And she
met a number of influential people, people like the cultivated
Mr. Fields, the Brandeises, and the artists and writers who
frequented their salons and the offices of *McClure's.*

Of all the people whom Willa Cather met during these

years, perhaps the most significant meeting for her was that which introduced her to the writer Sarah Orne Jewett. Miss Jewett admired Willa, who resembled her in many ways, but she began to feel that the younger writer's talent was going to seed. Her work for the magazine was taking too much of her time and energy, Miss Jewett felt, and, in a lengthy letter to her friend, she gave her some important advice. "You must find a quiet place," she said. "You must find your own quiet center of life and write from that. . . . To write and work on this level we must live on it—we must at least recognize it and defer to it at every step." Miss Cather delayed, but eventually she followed the advice, retired from *McClure's* and, revisiting the West, found her "quiet center of life." The result was *O Pioneers!*, the book with which she achieved greatness.

It had taken Willa Cather a long time to find her stride. She was forty when she wrote *O Pioneers!* But the book established her, as Ferris Greenslet remarked, "as a novelist of the first rank," a position which each of her ensuing books helped to buttress. She worked hard in the little apartment at 5 Bank Street, in Greenwich Village, that she and her close friend Edith Lewis now took. But she found much pleasure in the cultural activity of the city, which her freedom from routine employment gave her a greater opportunity to enjoy. The theater continued to enthrall her, but music became an even more important source of delight. In that golden age of the Metropolitan, she knew people like Louise Homer, Geraldine Farrar and Olive Fremstad. She was particularly inspired by the career of the latter singer, and her next book, *The Song of the Lark,* owes much to her friendship with Miss Fremstad.

Many of the short stories in *Youth and the Bright Medusa* are about the artists, writers and singers Miss Cather knew in New York. But in *My Ántonia* she returned to the West and to "the precious, the incommunicable past" for her theme. Ántonia seems "to mean to us the country, the conditions, the whole adventure of our childhood." But World War I cut short the adventure. In *One of Ours,* a Pulitzer prize-winning war novel published in 1922, Claude Wheeler, the young hero, is able to escape from the stultifying stupidity of a cramped, modern existence only through the violence of war. His army experiences take him abroad, away from the meanness and petty scheming that have dominated his environment and frustrated him. He comes to feel that "no battle field or shattered country he has seen was as ugly as this world would be if men like his brother Bayliss controlled it altogether." For Bayliss is like Ivy Peters of *A Lost Lady,* one of those people "who had never dared anything, never risked anything." Shrewd, calculating, trained to petty economics, they "root out the spirit of freedom, the generous, easy life . . ." And it seemed to Miss Cather as though these people had inherited the post-war world.

"The world," she was to say later, "broke in two in 1922 or thereabout." It had started to break long before. The events in *A Lost Lady* take place only a generation after the coming of the pioneers to the West. But already Neil Herbert, the departing narrator of the story, felt that "the people, the very country itself were changing so fast that there would be nothing to come back to." Willa Cather was not averse to change. She celebrated the opening of the frontier and the changes that came with the men who put it under "an iron harness." But she realized, as her biographer E. K. Brown points out, "that America was created not . . . by sheer vitality . . . but by a heroism alike sensitive and perceptive; that it took men and women of large imagination and unbending faith to achieve a pioneer greatness which a later generation accepted without comprehending."

The work of Willa Cather's later years was to uncover those people of large imagination and unbending faith who, like the Scandinavian immigrants of the Midwest, brought vital traditions to the new land. In *Death Comes for the Archbishop*, her finest novel, she finds them in the Southwest among "conical hills . . . the shape of Mexican ovens, red as brick dust, and naked of vegetation except for small juniper trees." She finds them in the shape of two French priests, quixotic, contemplative Bishop Latour and Father Vaillant, his vital, active Panza. And when she finds them the land is transformed as it was at *Agua Segreta*—Hidden Water— where, coming parched from the desert, Father Latour finds "running water, clover fields, cottonwoods, acacias, little adobe houses with brilliant gardens, a boy driving a flock of white goats toward the stream." For the seeds of tradition— in this case the Catholic faith—transform the land and the people. Implanted in the new land by early Spanish missionaries, they were nourished by these Frenchmen and bore fruit. It is true that the fruit is sometimes a strange, exotic growth. Transplanted fruit often is. But it is rich and nourishing nonetheless.

Miss Cather had become increasingly concerned with religion during her later years. She had been confirmed in the Episcopal church in 1922, and two of her late novels deal extensively and sympathetically with Catholicism. But despite this concern, Miss Cather realized that the religious tradition is not the only avenue of escape from pettiness. Nor is it the only place in which men of imagination—or faith—can be found. Euclide Auclair, the sceptical apothecary of *Shadows on the Rock*, rather shocks his young daughter Cécile sometimes by his failure to take her "miracles" seriously. But his imagination brings him to the new world and faith in himself and his intelligence keeps him from following the senseless contemporary practice of bleeding ill people whom he is called upon to treat. It is the tradition of sceptical reason that M. Auclair follows. Unlike his future son-in-law, Pierre Charron, however, he is unwilling to condemn the austerity of the religious life. It is true that such a life as that led by Jeanne le Ber, the recluse of Montreal, often produces suffering. Her father, the count, and Pierre, her intended husband, both suffer grievously through her actions. But Jeanne's visions are, perhaps, as real as anything man knows. And they provide solace and comfort not only for Jeanne, but for hunters and trappers, priests and nuns, merchants and farmers who have heard of her all over Canada.

The shadows of tradition that the Old World throws upon the rock in the St. Lawrence known as Quebec are many. Ours is not to question and condemn but to accept and live as we best can. For, like shadows, we must all soon pass. However, in her final novel, *Sapphira and the Slave Girl*, Miss Cather's shadows deepen and become sinister. There can be no question of toleration here. Slavery, like some aspects of religion, produces suffering. But it offers no compensation. It warps and limits even those people, like Sapphira, who stand to profit most from it. And the paternalistic protection which it offers to the docile is a denial of man's dignity that can be tolerated as little when it depends for its justification on the color of his skin as when it is based on his national origin or his place in the social scale.

Miss Cather ended her career as a novelist with *Sapphira and the Slave Girl*, published in 1940. She lived on for another seven years, but she wrote little during this period. Her time was devoted, principally, to music, reading and a circle of intimate friends, a circle gradually diminished by the frequent recurrence of death. Isabelle McClung had died some years before, and in 1945 her favorite brother Roscoe died.

Miss Cather herself was visited with illness. But more serious than any specific ailment was her loss of vital energy. Always an active woman, her new proneness to fatigue was particularly burdensome. Though she continued about her daily rounds, she was tired, worn out by work. And World War II, threatening to destroy the Old World that she had loved, added to her feeling of futility and despair. The end of the war brought a renewal of hope, and she was planning to begin writing again when death came, on April 24, 1947. She lies buried, as she wished, in the shadow of Mount Monadnock in Jaffrey, New Hampshire, but her spirit lives on in her novels. They are there, "heroic in size, a picture writing on the sun."

Carl Sandburg

CARL SANDBURG defined slang, that vivid idiom of the people so frequently condemned by school teachers and mothers, as "the language that takes off its coat, spits on its hands, and gets to work." He uses this sort of language in his poems. As a matter of fact, *The People, Yes,* one of his best known books of poetry, reproduces many of the phrases of the common people, the vividness of which we appreciate here, perhaps, for the first time. "Nohow classical," it seems to contain, like most of Sandburg's work, ". . . the roar and whirl of street crowds, work gangs, sidewalk clamor." For Carl Sandburg is a strong, bold writer, an experimenter in words and rhythms who is very much akin to his own concept of Chicago,

Flinging magnetic curses amid the toil of piling job on job, . . .
      a tall bold slugger set vivid against the little soft cities.

He, too, is

Laughing even as an ignorant fighter laughs who has never lost a
      battle.

Indeed, someone has called him the strong man's answer to
Whitman's question: "Do you suppose the liberty and brawn
of These States have to do only with delicate lady-words? With
gloved gentleman-words?" Having little to do with either the
words or the activities of ladies or gentlemen, he embodies the
beauty, the strength, the power, and some of the faults of the
people whom he portrays—the backbone and muscle of These
States.

His faults are, in part, a result of that humility which makes
him one with the nameless—though not voiceless—multitude
whom he celebrates. He says with them:

> All I know is what I hear.
> All I know is what I read in the papers.
> All I know you can put in a thimble.
> All I know I keep forgetting.

All too often, unfortunately, the limitation appears, to Sandburg and the nameless millions, to be no limitation at all but
a decided advantage. In a way, of course, it is just that. It is
not critical intelligence or self analysis that makes Chicago—
symbol of the new American industrial giant—

> Hog Butcher for the World
> Tool Maker, Stacker of Wheat
> Player with Railroads and the Nation's Freight Handler;
> Stormy, husky, brawling,
> City of the Big Shoulders.

Chicago is "proud to be alive and coarse and strong and cunning," and it is these characteristics that Sandburg celebrates
in his poems. His lyrics are songs of the sleeping tenements
and the sun-soaked cornfields. He finds America there and
in the steel, the great roaring factories, the quarries, and the
golden wheat fields that give strength to the people.

However, despite strength and cunning, hard times come and the jobs go. The butchers and tool makers, wheat stackers and freight handlers can't replenish their strength because they are duped by a more savage cunning. What happens then? Sandburg, along with the naïve and the unthinking, is thrown back on a pious hope.

> It's going to come out all right—do you know?
> The sun, the birds, the grass—they know
> They get along—and we'll get along.

But even grappling with a tenuous hope—perhaps then more than ever—the heroic proportions of the people and their spokesman are revealed:

In the darkness with a great bundle of grief the people march.
In the night, and overhead a shovel of stars for keeps, the people
    march:
        "Where to? What next?"

Brought into the world on a cornhusk mattress in a three-room frame house near the Chicago, Burlington and Quincy Railroad tracks in Galesburg, Illinois on January 6, 1878, Carl Sandburg learned the griefs and joys, the hopes and disappointments of the common people at an early age. He was the second child, his sister Mary having been born some three years earlier to the Swedish immigrant parents who had settled in this midwestern town. Five more brothers and sisters were to be born into the family before Carl was ten years old. Their first clothes, like his, were to be the diapers that their mother cut from Pillsbury flour sacks. As she cut and stitched for their younger brothers and sisters, the fair, strong little woman whom the children called "Mama" and the father called "Klawrah"—Swedish for Clara—often reminded the children that "in the old country we had *white* bread only at Easter and Christmas. Here in America," she would continue, "we have *white* bread every day in the year." And the sacks in which the flour came made good diapers. For the babies came along regularly, and money was scarce for working people even here in America.

And they were a working family. The father, August Sandburg, made only thirty-five dollars a month for working ten hours a day, fifty-two weeks a year as a helper in the C B and Q blacksmith shop in Galesburg. The serious, rather stern "black Swede," with straight black hair and dark eyes, whom young Carl called "Papa," was to raise a deforming hump of muscle on his back from pounding a heavy sledge on an anvil for ten hours a day. But he loved hard work and would come home from his job to dig in the large vegetable garden which he had planted or to make repairs on the ten-room house on Berrien Street that the family moved into when Carl was four years old.

This house was an important acquisition for the family. Some of the rooms were rented out to tenants, and among the working people who shared the Sandburg roof for varying periods of years were men like the solitary carpenter, Joe Elser, who told Carl about his soldiering during the Civil War and baked delicious pies. The rent of these tenants went toward the heavy burden of the mortgage on the house bought out of meager savings. Later there was legal trouble over an obscure clause in the mortgage that was to cost Carl's father almost a thousand hard-earned dollars. Young Carl, or "Sholly" as his father would call him, tells us that he had ten smiles from his mother for every one from his father. Perhaps it was this debt hanging over his head that made the father so serious. For he was so anxious to pay what he owed, to do his job, to get ahead and put a little by that he had little time for anything else. Unlike Carl's mother, he never learned to write. He read only a weekly Swedish-language paper and his Swedish Bible, and he was suspicious of the future poet's preoccupation with books. More than once he would say to the boy bent over some volume borrowed from the local library, "Sholly, you read too much in de books—what good iss it?"

Carl had few enough opportunities to read. In the endless repair work on the house, he was his father's helper, often holding a lantern for hours at a time while his father repaired a chair, put a new board in the floor, fixed the back fence, or replaced some missing shingles. And there were other jobs for the eldest son. In those days the kitchen, which was the only room in the house really heated during the cold months, served a family of nine as kitchen, dining room, study, playroom and workshop. It was heated by a coal stove which Carl stoked and emptied. Later he was to ask, good-naturedly, "Was it a thousand times or two thousand I pulled out that ashpan and opened the door to the back porch and went down the steps to the ends of the potato rows, where I dumped one more pan of ashes on the honorable Ashpile?"

The cry of "Charlie, the coal is gone" from the mother, or "Friskt vatten, Sholly" from the father, who sometimes fell back on Swedish, would send young Carl scampering outside to coal bin or pump for more coal or fresh water. Every couple of days there would be coffee to grind and lamps to fill. And in summer there would be bugs to pick and weeding to be done in the vegetable garden that supplied a major portion of the family's food.

It was not all work in the Sandburg household, however. There was corn to pop over the stove and taffy to pull. Nuts gathered in October were cracked on a flat iron with a hammer and eaten during the long winter months. Games were played. "Uncle Joe" Elser upstairs had his Civil War stories to tell. Like most boys, Carl and his brother Mart would snitch cookies and doughnuts from their mother's shelves, and they learned how to shinny over the transom into the cupboard where their father kept a barrel of eating apples. The large sheets of brown wrapping paper that came into the house on packages were saved. And it was on these carefully hoarded sheets that young Carl did his early drawing and writing.

For the young Sandburg baseball was more than a game: it was a passion. Before falling asleep at night he would imagine himself "sliding to second, sliding to third, and stealing home." During the day he played with the Berrien Street kids in a cow pasture, using a broom handle bat and a handmade ball. Later they got a regulation ball and made fielder's gloves out of ordinary man-sized gloves stuffed with cotton or hair.

There were other activities. The circus came to town, and Carl got up at four o'clock to water the elephants for a free ticket. The Knox County Fair was an event held annually in nearby Knoxville. Carl and his gang—the Dirty Dozen they called themselves—would always be there for it. Occasionally the boys got into trouble. They made too much noise playing duck-on-a-rock under the newly installed electric light at the corner of Day and Berrien streets and were chased by the neighbors. One hot summer day the whole gang was hauled through the streets in the open-topped patrol wagon and deposited in the Cherry Street calaboose for the afternoon. They had gone swimming without their clothes in the muddy pond known as the Old Brick, and some fussy old maid had complained to the police.

When there was nothing else to do, the gang would congregate in the back room at Schulz's cigar store. Here they would swap jokes and yarns, sing songs and invent nicknames for one another. Carl soon became "Cully," a name which old Galesburg friends still know him by. One of his best friends was "Frenchy" Juneau. And there were, among others, "Husky" Larsen, "Skinny" Seely, "Monk" Swanson, "Bullhead" Johnson, and, most curious of all, "Muffa de Grit Eddie" Rosenberg.

Young Carl Sandburg got his first regular job that paid him cash when he was eleven years old. At a quarter to eight every morning he would open the door of the Callender and Rodine real estate office, sweep out the room, and empty and clean the wide, round, flat brass spittoons, taking care to polish them once a month till they were bright and shiny. For this job he was paid, weekly, "twenty-five cents of United States money, a silver quarter of a dollar." Later he also got an afternoon job, delivering the *Galesburg Republican-Register* to fifty or sixty people for a dollar a week and a free copy of the paper, which he read diligently. "What with spading two or three gardens, picking a pail or two of potato bugs, selling Pennsylvania Grit along Main Street, and other odd jobs," he made, according to his autobiography, "about twelve dollars a month." Every penny of it was more than welcome in the Sandburg home, for hard times had come to Galesburg and his father was often working only half a day in the Q shops.

Though Carl enjoyed school and still remembers his early teachers with affection, his demonstrated ability to add to the limited income of the family helped him decide to interrupt his studies before he had reached high school. At fourteen he left school for a job, getting up at five-thirty to help the surly Mr. Burton on his milk delivery route. Since his father was working only part time, the money Carl made tided the family over and helped to see his sister Mary through high school. He read Mary's books, including Hawthorne's *Scarlet Letter,* which he detested, during his spare time.

It was while Carl was working for Mr. Burton that tragedy struck the family. Both Carl and his brother Mart had had sore throats that winter. Soon the two youngest brothers, Emil, aged seven, and two-year-old Freddy, had throats so sore that

they couldn't eat. When the doctor was called he diagnosed
the illness as the dreaded diptheria. Three days later both
brothers lay dead. They died in the narrow bed in the kitchen,
where they had been moved to benefit from the warmth of
the stove.

With the added expenses of medical and funeral bills, there
was no question of Carl's returning to school. But he did quit
the job with unfeeling Mr. Burton, who had not even a word
of consolation for the grief-stricken boy who had lost two
brothers. Carl worked for a while as assistant to Mr. Hineman,
the druggist, cleaning up, running errands and waiting on
the customers. He worked for another and more genial dairy
farmer with a milk route, reading in the delivery wagon as
the well-trained horse made its rounds. For a time he served
as porter and shoeshine boy in the barber shop under the
Farmer's and Mechanic's Bank. Here he got to see such celebrities as came to town and, in addition to his other duties,
scrubbed the backs of the men who could afford twenty-five
cents for a Saturday night bath in one of the barber shop's
eight public tubs.

Seeking to learn a trade, young Carl hired himself out to
a tinsmith. But his boss drank heavily and worked little and
Carl, seeing no future in the job, soon quit. The potter's trade
looked promising and interesting. Carl got a job as a "ball
pounder," preparing the clay for the skilled workmen who
shaped it on their wheels. But one night the pottery burned
down and Carl was out of work again.

He held a variety of jobs after that. He worked as water
boy on a construction job. He washed pop bottles in a bottling
plant. He carried water, ran errands, and sponged down horses
at the Williams racetrack. One summer he operated a refreshment stand and rowboat concession on nearby Lake George.
During the winter he worked as a night shift ice cutter on

the same lake, harvesting ice with much older and stronger men. But he had been touched by wanderlust. When he was eighteen he had taken a trip to Chicago, where he had lived for three days on the dollar-and-a-half that he had saved penny by penny for the trip. Now, a year later, he felt the urge to travel again. So one day in June, over the opposition of his parents and weighted down with the clothes on his back, "a small bar of soap, a razor, a comb, a pocket mirror, two handkerchiefs, a piece of string, needles and thread, a Waterbury watch, a knife, a pipe and a sack of tobacco, three dollars and twenty-five cents in cash," he hopped a westbound freight, hoping to get a look at the Mississippi River and willing to take whatever adventures came his way.

Four months later he was back in Galesburg. He had seen the Mississippi from the deck of a boat on which he had worked his passage down the river. He had also seen the Rocky Mountains, having picked pears for a dollar a day in their shadow. He had traveled as a "gaycat," working till he got a few dollars as a railroad section hand, short order cook, dish washer, stove blacker, wood chopper, or harvest hand and then moving on. He had been treated to "lumps," or free hand-outs, by kindly hobos and swindled out of his wages by crooked employers. He had been approached by a second-story man who wanted to take him on as an accomplice and beaten by a "shack" (hobo for brakeman) who wanted money for letting him bum a ride. He had met men who were mean, but he had also been with those who were open-hearted and gay. He had learned to sing and swap yarns, to think fast and speak freely. He had left Galesburg a restless boy, and he came back a mature young man with a new respect for himself and his fellow Americans.

Upon his return Sandburg apprenticed himself to a house painter, hoping to learn the trade. But that February the

Maine was blown up, and in April Carl was in uniform, on his way to Cuba and the Spanish-American War with the Sixth Infantry Regiment of the Illinois Volunteers. Sandburg quotes with approval Theodore Roosevelt's remark that "It wasn't much of a war but it was all the war there was." Young Carl didn't fire a shot, but he did pick up some Spanish and many body lice. He ate spoiled G.I. beef and was eaten by Cuban mosquitoes. He also had some letters from the island printed in the *Galesburg Evening Mail*. The war in Porto Rico, unlike most wars, was not very bloody. But like all wars, it was, in Sandburg's words, "a dirty and lousy affair while it lasted."

Sandburg had been a good soldier, however, and upon his return he was appointed to West Point. Despite his having missed high school, he passed spelling, geography and history examinations, failing only arithmetic and grammar. Apparently Douglas MacArthur, his classmate for two weeks, was more proficient in arithmetic.

Perhaps it was just as well that Sandburg's knowledge of long division and irregular verbs was incomplete, for, though he had done well in the ranks, the young friend of hobos and migratory workers would have been sorely chafed by the rigid caste system of the officer class.

He was happier at Lombard College, where he enrolled upon his return to Galesburg. He spent four years there, studying the classics with a Latin professor who milked his own cow and drove her to pasture before coming to class. In addition to attending classes Carl played basketball on the school team, joined the debating society, and was elected editor-in-chief of the college paper. He worked his way through four years of college by ringing the tower bell for classes, serving as janitor and, later, working as "call man" on the Galesburg fire department. Moreover, before Carl had left Lombard, his English teacher, Professor Wright, who was more interested in poetry than grammar, helped Carl publish his first book. Called *In Restless Ecstasy,* it was a collection of poetry and prose, lyrics and free verse, essays and random thoughts drawn from his experiences among working men, soldiers and tramps.

Carl Sandburg's feet began to itch and he left Lombard in his fourth year without taking a degree. He picked up the kit of "stereoscopic views" that he had peddled during his summer vacations and hit the road once more. He made enough peddling pictures to feed and clothe himself, and, since he was not interested in making a fortune, after he had "bagged a few orders he felt free a few days. Free to read, to observe men and things, and to think." He traveled as far west as the Rockies again and eastward to New York, selling his slides between stints on "various fugitive publications" and singing the songs he heard to the tune of his battered guitar.

In those days Wisconsin was a liberal state. When Sandburg's peregrinations brought him to Milwaukee in 1908, he saw something he liked and decided to stay for awhile. He was caught up by the fervor of a city that was not suspicious of intellectuals, whether they came from Harvard College or from Lombard. And he became a part of the movement for decent government and recognition of the rights of the working man. He settled down to work, writing for several newspapers, reading seriously, speaking for the men who were doing things for Wisconsin. Later he was to serve for two years as personal secretary to the man his activity helped to make mayor of Milwaukee, Emil Siedel. But in his first year in the city Carl spent most of his time with a pretty, slim brunette with a Phi Beta Kappa key from the University of Chicago. Her name was Lillian Steichen, but she was soon to be Mrs. Sandburg. They were married in June of 1908. Encouraged by his bride, Carl was soon spending the time he could snatch from newspaper and organizational work furiously writing poetry.

It was in these years and in the years immediately following, in Chicago, where he and his wife and baby daughter moved in 1912, that he was writing a poem a day. First drafts would be scribbled on the rough copy paper that he carried, reporter fashion, in his pocket. Ideas for poems would come to him as he sat at his desk in the office of one of the various newspapers for which he worked, or on the train, or at lunch, or while strolling in the street. He would jot them down as they came and then work over them—endlessly—at night, perfecting and refining. He was doing the work that was to result in four volumes of poetry in six short years.

The first of these volumes, *Chicago Poems,* was published in 1916. It sounded a new note in American poetry, a note of independence and vitality that had not been heard since Whitman's day. But then, as now, vitality and independence, often suspect, were offensive to some people. The slobbering roar of a furniture-wrecking preacher, paid by wealthy employers to keep the minds of discontented workers off their sordid lot, moved Sandburg to disgust. And in his poem *To a Contemporary Bunkshooter,* he voices this disgust, to the horror of some of his readers. But the qualms of the timid did not disturb Sandburg. Having the independence to stand up and voice the attitudes of himself and his fellow workers, he could go,

Bragging and laughing that under his wrist is the pulse, and under
     his ribs the heart of the people,
          Laughing!

By the time Sandburg's second volume, *Cornhuskers,* appeared in 1918, another daughter had come to join his first-born. And his power and feeling are restrained and refined in an attempt to interpret the silent mysteriousness of nature.

There is a mystical, almost spiritual quality in *Prairie,* the first poem in the volume, and this quality pervades the book, to the surprise of readers of the earlier, more pugnacious Sandburg. The poignant lyricism of *Cool Tombs,* with its evocation of Lincoln and Pocahontas, and the soft, whispering, care-effacing music of *Grass* are typical of this later poetry. In direct contrast to the robust two-fistedness of the first volume, he has here perceived and recreated a quiet, delicate beauty.

Poetry writing was interrupted, briefly, for Sandburg by World War I. At forty-two he was too old to serve in the army. But he did go abroad as a foreign correspondent, his knowledge of Swedish making him extremely useful in Stockholm. Upon his return, in 1919, he took up with the *Chicago Daily News,* a paper with which he remained for thirteen years. His sympathetic understanding of the working man made him an excellent commentator upon the labor scene in and around Chicago. One series of articles that he wrote during these years dealt with the garment trades. In these articles he showed how the cooperation between management and labor in that industry brought advantages to both, and how such an enlighted policy might provide a pattern for the nation to follow. Another, less happy, experience was that described in a series of articles later collected and published as *The Chicago Race Riots,* a frightening picture of a city swept by hate brought on by insecurity. Sad to relate, the entire episode might never have occurred had a few greedy men been forced to curb their lust for greater gain.

While working for the *News* Carl returned to his poetry. *Smoke and Steel,* an amplification and an integration of many of the elements of his earlier verse in a mature synthesis, was published in 1920. It was followed by *Slabs of the Sunburnt West,* another volume of verse, in 1922.

With his family, his newspaper work, and his poetry, Sandburg was busy enough to have worn out several less energetic men. But he added another interest. Biography had intrigued him since boyhood days. Back in Galesburg he had tracked down several men who smoked Duke's cigarettes and talked them into saving for him the vest pocket cigarette biographies that came in their packs. At Lombard his interest had crystallized, and he read everything pertaining to Lincoln that he could lay his hands on. One of the famous Lincoln-Douglas debates had been held on the Lombard College campus, and there were men in town who could still recall the event. Sandburg talked to the men and remembered their impressions. Over the years he collected Lincoln material. Now he began to mull over his collection. He classified, arranged, formulated and discarded material, involved in a project that would come to fruition several years hence.

Meanwhile, his family had grown, too. He had three daughters now, and two of them were at the tell-me-a-story age. Deeply rooted in America himself, he found that most of the children's stories he knew were pale and artificial imitations of European models. "I was tired of princes and princesses," he says. "I wanted something more in the American lingo." So he wrote those wonderful "nonsense tales with American fooling in them," the *Rootabaga Stories*. Full of such tales as those about the Zig Zag Railroad, Hot Dog the Tiger, the Village of Cream Puffs, and the two skyscrapers who wanted to have a child, the two volumes are as American as Coney Island or an ice cream cone. His children, and thousands of others, were delighted.

Equally delighted were many other thousands, people who had never read a line of Sandburg's poetry, when he produced *The American Songbag* in 1927. The book is a collection of the songs Sandburg had heard on the lips of railroad men, cowboys, lumberjacks, hobos, convicts, and workers on farm and in factory as he traveled up and down the country, in his earlier years, with his guitar, or "gittar" as he pronounces it, and his peddler's pack. In it are the love songs and laments, the work songs, spirituals and jig tunes of singing America.

The Lincoln story that Sandburg had been thinking about for years first began to take shape in his mind as another story for children. But he soon discovered that the material was too complex to be simplified for young readers without distortion or the omission of much relevant information. Consequently, he revised his original plan and went back to work on a full-length biography. *Abraham Lincoln: The Prairie Years,* published in 1926, was the result of that work. In the two volume's 962 pages Sandburg traces Lincoln's life from his birth in his father's crude log cabin to his departure fifty-two years later for the White House and his first term as President of the United States. Lincoln is seen here through the eye of the historian, who presents the man against a detailed background of his times. Sandburg had spent years digging up information, ferreting out facts to which the portrait is strictly faithful. The legend of Lincoln is dissipated by Sandburg the historian. And Lincoln the man emerges, more heroic for his humanity than the faultless plaster saint that legend had drawn. But it is not the historian's eye alone that looks at Lincoln. The book is a great human document as well as an accurate historical one because Sandburg has looked at Lincoln with the penetrating vision of the poet, a poet who knew from experience what it was to grow up, a poor boy among working people, in a prairie state.

The children's book of Sandburg's original plan was to be written later. Drawn from *The Prairie Years, Abe Lincoln Grows Up* (1931) is a straightforward account of Lincoln's youth written for young Americans. The popularity of the book is attested to by the fact that its author, according to his wife, was sought out by visiting children, when he lived in Chicago, as often as were the stockyards.

Two more books of verse, *Good Morning America* (1928) and *The People, Yes* (1936), were written during this period, as well as a biography of Sandburg's brother-in-law, *Steichen the Photographer*.

But Lincoln continued to dominate Sandburg's thoughts. There were the years in Washington to be accounted for, years of anguish and ultimate victory for the man and the nation. Sandburg had evolved a curious filing system for his material while working on *The Prairie Years*. He had labeled one envelope "Looks," and into it he stuffed every bit of available information on Lincoln's appearance. Another was marked "Gettysburg Speech," and in it went notes and comments on that famous event. There was a folder devoted to Lincoln's laughter, another on religion, one for each Civil War battle, yet another on the White House while Lincoln occupied it. And all of these envelopes, piled in orange crates in the attic where Sandburg worked, were bulging with unused material. In addition, there were books: early biographies of Lincoln, lives of men in his cabinet and army, volumes of Congressional records—there were 133 volumes in a single set of *Official Records of the Rebellion* alone. The overflow from his shelves filled a barn at "Chickaming," the place on the shores of Lake Michigan that the Sandburgs bought before Carl retired from the newspaper business in 1932. Looking back on his plan to condense all of this material into three or four summary chapters to be added to his published work on Lincoln, Sandburg now exclaims, "There was valor in my innocence!"

So vitally important a part of Lincoln and America could not be condensed. At the age of fifty, therefore, Sandburg started the enormous task of completing his biography of Lincoln. Before he had finished he had produced more volumes—over a million words—constituting the most authoritative, lively and interesting re-creation of a man and a statesman ever produced in this country. The work was called *Abraham Lincoln: The War Years.* In it Sandburg traces Lincoln's career from the time of his departure for the White House, the point at which he had left him in *The Prairie Years,* to May 4, 1865, when a procession of mourners ". . . lavished heaps of fresh flowers as though there never could be enough to tell either their hearts or his."

> And the night came with great quiet.
> And there was rest.
> The prairie years, the war years, were over.

Carl Sandburg's career as a writer, however, was not over with the completion of his monumental biography of Lincoln. *Abraham Lincoln: The War Years,* in four volumes, was awarded the Pulitzer Prize in 1939. At the age of sixty-five he began his first novel, *Remembrance Rock,* which he spent five years upon and published in 1948. In 1950 Mr. Sandburg again received the Pulitzer Prize, this time for his work, *Complete Poems.* At the age of seventy-five, he published *Always the Young Strangers,* a volume of autobiography which Robert E. Sherwood calls "the best autobiography ever written by an American." And he adds: "I am not forgetting Benjamin Franklin or Henry Adams, nor showing them disrespect." Since *Always the Young Strangers* traces Sandburg's life only to the beginning of his college days, perhaps we can hope for further volumes dealing with his later career, a career of tremendous vitality and almost infinite variety. Speaking of that career in "Notes for a Preface," the humble man of the people who had been experimenting with words for most of his long life says, "All my life I have been trying to learn to read, to see and hear, and to write. . . . I should like to think that as I go on writing there will be sentences truly alive, with verbs quivering, with nouns giving color and echoes. It could be, in the grace of God," he continues, "I shall live to be eighty-nine, as did Hokusai, and speaking my farewell to earthly scenes, I might paraphrase: 'If God had let me live five years longer I should have been a writer.' "

Sinclair Lewis

SINCLAIR LEWIS, the man who put Main Street on the map, was the first American author to be awarded the Nobel prize for literature. He was born in 1885, in Sauk Center, Minnesota, a town much like the Gopher Prairie of *Main Street*. In Lewis's youth Sauk Center was a small prairie village, "a town of a few thousand in a region of wheat and corn and dairies and little groves." It was here, in a country largely inhabited by Scandinavian immigrants, that Dr. Edwin J. Lewis, himself the son of a Connecticut country doctor, came to start his practice upon graduation from medical school. He married Emma Kermott, who died shortly after the birth of Sinclair, her third son. Her husband remained, carrying on his practice. Already, like Doc Vickerson in *Arrowsmith*, he had been too long in Sauk Center to be known as anything but "Ole Doc Lewis." His third son became, quite naturally, "Ole Doc Lewis's youngest boy," or "Claude Lewis's red-headed kid brother."

Lewis's boyhood, as he describes it, was commonplace enough: "lessons in school, swimming in summer, hunting ducks in the autumn, skating in winter, with such household tasks as sawing stove-wood and cleaning from the sidewalk the deep snow of the far northern land." The one unusual pastime in that small town that he admits to was reading. He delighted in Dickens, Scott, and Washington Irving. His stepmother, a kindly woman whom his father married when the boy was six, read to him "more than was the village custom." And he had access to the three or four hundred volumes, exclusive of medical books, in his father's library—volumes his father had collected as a schoolteacher before he went to medical school. The medical texts were not ignored, of course. With their color plates "depicting the awful intimacies of the innards," they were the books he "sneaked the gang in to behold and shiver over" when the Doctor was off on a Case.

However, it was Claude, about five years older than his young brother and "a hustler," who was the leader of the gang. Sinclair, or "Harry" (sometimes "Hal") as he was called through his college days, was, by his own confession, "a skinny, perpetually complaining small boy." He had little to do with his older brother, Fred, who was "given to fishing and meditation." But Claude was always up to something, and Harry, after the manner of pesky younger brothers, always tagged along. He would, of course, have his clothes tied in knots and soaked when he followed the gang to "the swimming-hole in Hoboken Crick." But as this did not deter him, one of the gang was deputed to lose Harry when an expedition was planned. He soon became an expert at the job, and Harry was often left behind to return to his books when the gang went off on a jaunt.

Perhaps it was his early interest in books, or perhaps it was his desire to over-awe with "strictly high-class intellectual feats" the boys who outshone him in diving, skating, shooting prairie chickens, and catching fish through a hole in the ice that started young Harry on his newspaper career. In any case, one summer when he was about fifteen years old he got a part-time job with Mr. Hendryx, editor of the weekly Sauk Center *Herald*. His primary responsibility was sweeping out the office, and his pay was nothing a week. But he was learning typesetting, and he was soon being bribed with cup cakes by members of the women's club anxious to have their names in print. Before the summer was over he was proficient enough to set short news items directly in type without writing them out. At this point he asked for a raise but got fired instead.

He was undaunted, however, and the following summer he got a job with the other paper in town, the Sauk Center *Weekly Avalanche*. Here he was paid the munificent sum of three dollars a week for "merely sweeping, reporting, setting type, running the hand press, and rushing the growler." In later years Lewis thought that he had probably been overpaid at that. But he did discover, while "giving the world his Message and trying to keep ink off his blouse," that it was not only schoolteachers who were "fanatics about commas and 'they was.'" He had already learned the first rule of writing: "If you have always seen a statement made in a certain way, that is itself a reason for not saying it that way."

Lewis attended the ordinary local public schools, and upon his graduation from high school he spent a couple of months at Oberlin College, in Ohio. His father, however, was a country doctor of greater education than was common in those days. He was, moreover, from Connecticut, and as a former schoolteacher he was aware of the value of education. Despite his meager income as a small town general practitioner, he determined to send his youngest son to Yale. Young Harry made his first trip to the East Coast and a new life with gratitude and expectation in his heart. The gratitude was to remain always. The expectation prompted him to send his trunk on to New Haven from Albany, while he took a Hudson River Day Boat down the river for his first glimpse of fabulous Manhattan. This, for a young man who had delighted in Washington Irving, was "to swim into New York on a tide of history." Contemporary New York was less satisfying than the historic Hudson Valley, however. Arriving in the city just as the evening commuters to Jersey piled into the ferry slip, he was scared stiff by the crowds. This was in 1903!

New Haven was quieter, and Yale was hospitable to the young freshman from the Midwest. He came under the benign influence of men like William Lyon Phelps—"Billy" Phelps to scores of Yale men. Thirty-one years after Lewis had left Yale, where he took all of Phelps' courses that he could, he looked back affectionately upon Billy as "the greatest of teachers, as well as the most agreeable of companions." Of course, not all of his teachers were like Phelps. He could recall, for instance, a short story class whose teacher "might have been harmful if he had only been brighter." And though Lewis contributed to both the *Yale Literary Magazine* and the *Courant* and had some of his early work published outside of school, the great realist was to remember his early literary productions as pieces "reeking with banal romanticism."

Literary and academic work did not use up all of the restless young man's energy. He was still interested in newspaper work, and he "toyed," as he expressed it, "one evening a week on the New Haven *Journal and Courier*." During summer vacations he traveled. One summer he went to England on a cattle boat. Another year, dissatisfied with college, he went to Panama in search of a job on the canal. From the latter trip he returned to New York as a stowaway, broke, having failed to get the job.

Perhaps more important to the future writer than any of these experiences was the sojourn at Helicon Hall. Helicon

Hall was a large old establishment on the Palisades in Engle-wood, New Jersey, which Upton Sinclair had secured for a group of serious young intellectuals attempting an experi-ment in communal living. In theory, the members of the group were to support themselves by working six or seven hours a day, devoting their leisure time to science, philosophy, art, and literature. Lewis, joining the group, like Hawthorne at Brook Farm before him, expected to find there a richer and intenser life. Like Hawthorne, he was disappointed. For Lewis, unused to manual labor, worked closer to seventeen hours a day than six. The furnace, which he was supposed to tend, was a bewildering array of hissing pipes and valves which he could not get to function properly. And the extra jobs he was asked to tackle were also beyond his scope. Nor were the other intellectuals adequate as cooks, laundresses, carpenters or house maids. Moreover, the leisure that was to have been devoted to intellectual matters was occupied with business or just plain loafing. And Lewis noticed that Upton Sinclair, who had talked him into joining the group by extoll-ing the value of manual labor, let the axe with which he chopped down trees rust unless there was a newspaper re-porter or a new young disciple to observe his displays of energy. After a month of Helicon Hall Lewis went back to Yale.

After graduating from Yale, Lewis worked for a short time on an Iowa newspaper and as a Night Agent for a New York City charity organization with the resounding title of Joint Application Bureau of the Charity Organization Society and the Association for the Improvement of the Condition of the Poor. Though he got to see a great deal of what has been re-ferred to as "the seamy side of life" in the latter job, he didn't feel that he was doing much about ameliorating the condi-tion of the poor. When he received a telegram from California offering him a job as secretary to two sisters who were collaborating on a book, he was glad to leave. The sisters—Alice Macgowan and Grace Macgowan Cook—had been told about Lewis by a former classmate at Yale, William Rose Benét. Lewis went West and spent several months sharing a shack with Benét in that writers' Paradise, Carmel-by-the-Sea. His job left him plenty of free time to write and loaf beside the crescent bay.

In that pleasant bucolic bohemia he soon became restless, however. He was off next to San Francisco and a job on the *Evening Bulletin.* More interested in writing a literary masterpiece than in getting names spelled correctly and facts straight, Lewis was not very successful as a reporter. But while working the hotel beat he did turn in one masterly bit of reporting. It was about a bellboy who had been kind to an old lady and had inherited her entire seventy-five thousand dollar estate when she died. There was only one thing wrong with the story. It wasn't true. It had been given to Lewis by an opportunistic hotel manager interested in getting his hotel's name into the paper. The manager had been using variations on that same tale for years, and he had an album full of clippings to show for his efforts.

Soon after delivering himself of this scoop Lewis was out of work again. And back across the continent he came. In Washington, D.C., he got a job as junior editor of *The Volta Review,* a journal for teachers of the deaf. He knew less about the subject, he later confessed, than he did "of radar, even though radar had not yet been invented." But he lasted for about a year before he left for New York again.

In New York Lewis met Grace Hegger, whom he married in 1914. He supported her and their young son, Wells— named after H. G. Wells, the novelist—by a series of "typical white-collar, unromantic, office literary jobs with two publishing houses, a magazine (*Adventure*), and a newspaper syndicate." He was merely marking time, waiting until he should be selling enough stories to magazines to be able to live by free-lancing. He was also writing novels. *Our Mr. Wrenn, The Trail of the Hawk, The Job, The Innocents* and *Free Air* were all published between 1914 and 1919. But they were uninspired, "dead before the ink was dry," as Lewis commented.

Disgusted with his work, Lewis decided to abandon conventional themes and write a book to please himself. No longer concerned with popular success, he attacked the treasured myth "that all American villages were peculiarly noble and happy." Tearing off the veils of sentimentality, hypocrisy and cant that covered most pictures of American life, he showed us, in *Main Street*, what we were really like. For, as Lewis says in his prologue, "Main Street is the continuation of Main Streets everywhere." And to eyes undimmed by sentiment it is a singularly distressing spectacle. With its clutter of cheap shops, its ugly public buildings, its houses—"meek cottages or large, comfortable, soundly uninteresting symbols of prosperity"—it seemed impossible that the citizens of Gopher Prairie could have thought it "either desirable or possible to make this, their common home, amusing or attractive." And the citizens themselves; what were they like? Bound by rigid conventions, torn by petty jealousies, smothered in smugness, coarse, stupid and intolerably dull, they were as unlike the romantic picture of the generous, open, democratic American as they could be. *Main Street* is an indictment of pioneer America gone to seed.

Surprisingly enough, Lewis's candid picture of America with its shoes off and its suspenders showing was a tremendous success. Though it scandalized stolid citizens, it sold 500,000 copies and made Lewis famous. Commenting on its popularity, Lewis claimed that the book was read "with the same masochistic pleasure that one has in sucking an aching tooth." Lewis continued his embarrassingly detailed documentation of American life with *Babbitt,* in 1922. Investigating suburbia, he turned here from Gopher Prairie to Zenith, a city patterned on Minneapolis, and George F. Babbitt, a member of the prosperous middle class whose standardized, advertised wares are "his symbols and proofs of excellence; at first the signs, then the substitutes, for joy and passion and wisdom."

With the publication of *Main Street* and *Babbitt,* Lewis, a gangling, long-legged man in his late thirties, became a figure of stormy controversy. The storm did not abate when, upon completing *Arrowsmith* a few years later, he was awarded the Pulitzer prize for fiction, the most coveted of American literary honors. For the independent redhead from Sauk Center had the integrity—the conservatives called it temerity—to refuse the prize. It was awarded annually "for the American novel published during the year which shall best present the wholesome atmosphere of American life, and the highest standard of American manners and manhood." Lewis could not wink at the terms and accept the award under false pretenses, so he rejected it altogether.

Arrowsmith, a book about the trials and frustrations of a scientist whose work is hampered by conventional social practices, was as carefully documented and replete with factual details as Lewis's earlier works. So careful was Lewis about details that he asked Dr. Paul De Kruif, the distinguished scientist, to check the scientific aspects of the book for him. The collaboration proved successful, and Lewis called upon experts for technical advice in other books. In *Elmer Gantry,* for instance, the Reverend L. M. Birkhead advised him on details of clerical life. But this book, attacking the well protected evil of the unscrupulous clergyman, did not receive the plaudits that *Arrowsmith* had won. As a matter of fact, a New England divine tried to have Lewis jailed for maligning the ministry. And a preacher from the West invited Lewis to come out and be lynched.

Honors were to come to Lewis, however. The year following the publication of *Dodsworth,* the story of an American Captain of Industry, he was chosen as the recipient of the Nobel Prize for Literature, the first American to be so honored. There were no distressing terms to qualify the award, and Lewis did not refuse it. But his address to the Swedish Academy was more annoying to certain of his cautious countrymen than a refusal would have been. For he accepted the award, humbly, as the representative of a new generation of American writers—artists like Cather, Dreiser, O'Neill, Sandburg, Hemingway, and Faulkner—who had broken with the genteel tradition. And he attacked the near-sighted American academicians who had failed to recognize the importance of these people. "Red" Lewis, despite his new dignity as a Nobel prize winner, was still a controversial figure.

Lewis had been divorced from his first wife in 1925. In England on one of his many travels, he met Dorothy Thompson, the well-known American newspaper correspondent and, according to mutual friends, "the only human being who could talk Lewis down." They were married in 1928, and, though they traveled extensively, an old Vermont farm which they bought and reconditioned became their chief residence. It was this New England environment that provided Lewis with the background for his last major work, *It Can't Happen Here.* This book, written in 1935, sounded a harsh note of warning against the dangers of an imminent American fascism.

Lewis did not stop writing after *It Can't Happen Here.* Far from it! But though he was tremendously prolific, the quality of his work was always uneven. One critic has called him "one of the most plunging and erratic writers in our literary history." He continued to experiment with new themes. *Kingsblood Royal,* for instance, is a courageous exploration of some of the problems of the Negro. One of his last books, *The God Seeker,* is a not very successful first attempt at a historical novel. But books like *Bethel Merriday, Gideon Planish* and *Cass Timberlane* seem to have been written with the moving pictures and popular magazines too much in mind. And *The Prodigal Parents* is so rankly conservative and uninspired that it might have been written by George F. Babbitt rather than by his creator.

Perhaps some of the faults of Lewis's later works can be attributed to unfortunate personal experiences. He was suffering from a serious skin disease which irritated a temper already notoriously short. Restless, he traveled extensively and overworked himself. Though he was writing a novel every year or two and serving as book editor of a national magazine, he became seriously interested in the theater in his later years. He enjoyed some success as actor-director in an adaptation of his novel, *It Can't Happen Here,* but the extra work and the excitement taxed his energy. And in the theater, as elsewhere, his restlessness and his irritability alienated friends and left him feeling empty and alone. In 1942 his second marriage ended in divorce, his wife retaining custody of their young son Michael. After the separation, Lewis drifted aimlessly, buying houses in which to settle down and then restlessly moving on. But the hardest blow of all for Lewis was the death of his son Wells in World War II. This child of his first marriage had had a brilliant career at Yale and, having published a first novel, showed signs of exceptional ability as a writer at his death.

Small wonder that the satiric impulse that had informed

Sinclair Lewis's earlier works was frittered away in petty squabbles and carping criticism or that, in his loneliness, sentimentality found its way into his later books. What is remarkable is that he was able to write at all under such circumstances. But write he did, until he died, alone in a hospital in Rome, on January 10, 1951. Though he was only sixty-six at his death, he had long been a sick, lonely old man. But despite the bitterness and the increasing conservatism of his later years, the man who wrote *Main Street* and *Babbitt* will always be remembered. For he not only "lodged a piece of a continent in the world's imagination," but also pointed the way toward a more realistic appraisal of American life for a whole generation of writers.

Eugene O'Neill

EUGENE O'NEILL . . . has done nothing much in American drama save to transform it utterly, in ten or twelve years, from a false world of neat and competent trickery to a world of splendor and fear and greatness . . . he has seen life as not to be neatly arranged in the study of a scholar but as a terrifying, magnificent and often quite horrible thing akin to the tornado, the earthquake, the devastating fire." In these words before the Swedish Academy on the occasion of his acceptance of the Nobel prize, Sinclair Lewis praised his fellow American, the dramatist who six years later was himself to win the coveted literary award, the second American to be so honored. Lewis, in his address, did justice to the great American dramatic artist. For O'Neill, coming upon an empty scene, had single-handedly created an American drama. But he was more than a pioneer pushing back the horizons of a provincial theater. His best dramas challenge comparison with the tragedies of the greatest of his European contemporaries.

Eugene Gladstone O'Neill, might be said to have been born into the theater. Son of James O'Neill, the actor, he was born on Broadway—in the Barrett House, at Forty-third Street, New York, on October 16, 1888. Season after season, his enormously successful father "cleared fifty thousand" touring the country in the melodramatic play, *Monte Cristo*. His mother, Ella Quinlan O'Neill, like her husband a devout Irish Catholic, accompanied the matinee idol, James, on his road tours. For the first seven years of his life Eugene trouped along with his parents, getting his fingers into grease paint and absorbing the life backstage. Later he was sent to a Catholic boarding school, or rather a series of such schools, for the rigid discipline of these institutions brought out the nonconformist in the boy and he was considered "a problem" by school officials.

Finishing his preparatory schooling at Betts Academy in Stamford, Connecticut, he entered Princeton in the fall of 1906. But his career at Princeton was a short one. In June of that year he was suspended for having, according to legend, thrown a beer bottle through the window of Woodrow Wilson, then President of the college.

His father having an interest in a cheap, mail-order jewelry business in New York, O'Neill got a job with the firm. He was married in 1909 to Kathleen Jenkins. But neither a white collar job answering the letters of mail-order customers nor the settled life of a married man could satisfy the restless youth. He left for Honduras to prospect for gold before his son, Eugene, Jr., was born the following year. The marriage, which was "a mistake" for both partners, was terminated by divorce in 1912.

In Honduras O'Neill found neither gold nor adventure, but fever. Invalided back home, he was put to work by his father as assistant manager of the company in which he was touring. But parental discipline proved as distasteful to the young man as the regularity demanded by a job and a wife.

Having read some of Conrad's tales, he decided to taste the romance of the sea and shipped as an ordinary seaman on a Norwegian barque bound for Buenos Aires.

In South America he drifted from job to job while ashore, working in turn for the Westinghouse, Swift, and Singer companies. Irked by the menial details of these shore jobs, he left one after another. He shipped on a cattle steamer, tending mules from Buenos Aires to Durban, South Africa in the stinking hold of the vessel. Returning to Buenos Aires, he hung around the waterfront during the day, making friends with sailors and outcasts like himself. At night he went to the Sailor's Opera, a waterfront café where he listened to sailors' yarns of adventure, "drank, played cards, fought and wallowed." He was soon completely destitute. After spending some time "on the beach," he signed as an ordinary seaman on a British tramp steamer bound for New York.

Back in New York, O'Neill lived at "Jimmy the Priest's," a waterfront dive, "with a back room where you could sleep with your head on the table if you bought a schooner of beer." The place got its name from the proprietor, "Jimmy," a man who, with his "pale, thin, clean-shaven face, mild blue eyes and white hair, seemed to be more suited for a cassock than the bartender's apron he wore." Transformed into "Johnny the Priest's," the saloon was later to serve O'Neill as the setting for the first act of *Anna Christie*, his Pulitzer prize-winning play. But at this point in his life there was no thought of prizes, or even of plays. O'Neill was down and out. He shared a vermin-infested three-dollar-a-month room over the saloon with another down-and-outer. He shared it, that is, until his roommate committed suicide by jumping from the window.

Hanging around the waterfront, O'Neill picked up occasional jobs as a seaman. He sailed on a mailboat. He shipped to Southampton, England, on the liner *New York* and returned on the *Philadelphia.* After the latter trip he won a considerable sum gambling and went on a wild party. When the spree was over he found himself "on a through train with a ticket for New Orleans."

Presenting himself to his father, who was completing a tour of the Southern circuit in *Monte Cristo,* O'Neill appealed for funds. But his father was tired of helping him out of scrapes and refused to give him the money. He offered him instead a chance to join the troupe as an actor and earn his money. The son, having exhausted his winnings, was forced to accept the job. Learning his small part on the train, he appeared for the first time as an actor at the company's next stop, in Ogden, Utah. O'Neill completed the fifteen-week tour with the company and returned with his parents to their home in New London. But he had not enjoyed the experience. *Monte Cristo* was a bombastic and artificial romance. And at one point in the tour when his father had complained, "Sir, I am not satisfied with your performance," O'Neill is said to have replied, "Sir, I am not satisfied with your play."

Upon his return to New London in August, 1912, Eugene got a job as a cub reporter on the New London *Telegraph.* For nearly six months he did regular reporting and contributed verses to a weekly column. Then, in December, the irregular life he had led claimed its toll. His health suddenly broke down, and it was discovered that he had a slight touch of tuberculosis. On Christmas Eve he entered the sanatorium at Gaylord Farm in Wallingford, Connecticut, for five months of complete rest. In the late spring he was discharged from the sanatorium, his case "arrested." The episode had been a brief one, but it marked a turning point in O'Neill's life. For while at the sanatorium he had been forced, in his idleness, to examine his experiences, "to digest and evaluate the impressions of many past years in which one experience had crowded on another with never a second's reflection." The consequences of this self-analysis were of staggering importance for the man and for the American theater.

Upon his release, O'Neill returned to his parents' home in New London. When his father went on tour a few months later, Eugene went to stay with the Rippins, a family of English friends with a home on Long Island Sound. He remained with his friends for over a year, restoring himself to health by getting a maximum amount of sunshine, outdoor exercise, and rest. Following the doctor's advice, he slept outdoors and went swimming in the Sound every day, winter and summer alike. Having determined to become a playwright while at the sanatorium, he filled his hours of rest with long-neglected reading, becoming "a voracious reader of plays." Later he was to comment, "I read about everything I could lay hands on: the Greeks, the Elizabethans—practically all the classics—and of course all the moderns." He had also begun to write, and before he had left the Rippins he published, with the financial assistance of his father, a book called *Thirst and Other One-Act Plays.*

Though O'Neill had had some experience as a writer, he discovered while writing his plays that he needed technical advice. A friend who read his first book, which was not a commercial success, suggested that he seek help in Cambridge. Accordingly, in the fall of 1914 O'Neill enrolled in Professor George Pierce Baker's "47 Workshop" class at Harvard. Bored though he must have been by the discussion of rudiments so imperative for the beginners in the class, O'Neill got a great deal from Professor Baker. Commenting later upon the value of the class, O'Neill said that ". . . the technical points, the analysis of the practice of playmaking . . . were . . . of inestimable value to us in learning our trade." But more important than the technical advice or the plays he wrote while in

"47" was the encouragement he received from Baker. Years later, looking back to Baker and the Workshop, O'Neill said: "The most vital thing for us, as possible future artists and creators . . . was to believe in our work and to keep on believing. He helped us to hope." An outcast and an apparent failure, O'Neill, more than anyone, needed that hope if he was to continue with his work.

Through with Harvard, O'Neill spent several months in Greenwich Village, New York. Then, in the summer of 1916, he went to Provincetown. Here, swimming and sunning himself on the sand, O'Neill met the members of the group later to be known as the Provincetown Players. They had acted in Provincetown during the preceding summer, and were back to experiment with drama again. George Cramm Cook, "Jig" to the Players, was the inspiring genius of the group, and he was eager to put on a play more vital than any that could be found in the tradition-bound commercial theater. O'Neill had a whole trunk full of his plays in the shack on the beach that he shared with a friend. When they were read by the enthusiastic group, two were scheduled for immediate production. As a result, *Bound East for Cardiff*, the first of O'Neill's plays to be seen on any stage, was produced in the Wharf Theatre, a converted fishing shack on the Provincetown wharf, with room for ninety people "if they didn't mind sitting close together on wooden benches with no backs." The night of the production, with O'Neill himself playing the part of the Second Mate, was as foggy as the night described in the play. "The tide was in," one of the actors recalls, "and it washed under us and around, spraying through holes in the floor." O'Neill's early sea plays could have had no more appropriate stage than the old Wharf Theatre.

Nor could the interpreters of O'Neill's plays have been more sympathetic. They produced *Thirst* as the fourth bill of their summer season, O'Neill again appearing in the cast of his own play. And when they returned to New York in the fall, now officially incorporated as the Provincetown Players, O'Neill and his plays went with them. In a converted brownstone-front house on Macdougal Street in New York's Greenwich Village, and later in a remodeled stable farther up the street, all of O'Neill's early plays and many of his later ones were produced by the Players. One of the group remarked years later that O'Neill had had "our Playwright's Theatre and our experimental stage to use always precisely as he wished to use them. . . . No other American playwright," she justly continued, "has ever had such prolonged preliminary freedom with stage and audience alike."

This prolonged freedom to experiment paid off when, with the publication of *Beyond the Horizon* in 1920, O'Neill won his first Pulitzer Prize. He had become by this time America's leading playwright. He had also remarried, in 1918. And his wife, the former Agnes Boulton, bore him another son and a daughter. His years as a roving outcast were over. Even his father, an old hand in the theater, recognized his ability and is reported to have wept at a performance of *Beyond the Horizon*. After the performance, however, the veteran trouper of the old-fashioned romantic theater is said to have asked the author of the modern drama of frustration if he was "trying to send the audience home to commit suicide."

Success did not go to O'Neill's head. Always extremely shy, he avoided the celebrity hunters who had begun to seek him out, and he retired to the country to write. In the morning he would work, rising early and writing from 8:30 to 1:30 in a script so tiny that people unfamiliar with his penmanship often need a magnifying glass to decipher it. Afternoons he would devote to outdoor exercise, remembering his breakdown and the necessity of looking after his health. In the sum-

mer he often retired to a lonely, reconditioned life-saving sta-
tion at Peakéd Hill, near Provincetown. Here he could work
without interruption. When he got tired he would go for a
long swim or round the point in the little Eskimo kayak which
he took out even in the roughest weather.

His long hours of work produced a series of extremely successful plays during this period. *The Emperor Jones,* based on
a story O'Neill had heard from a circus hand and depicting the
disintegration of character in a strong man beset by fear, was
produced in 1920. O'Neill here uses the first of many remarkable devices he was to employ in the theater. A drum similar
to those used in the jungles where the action of the play takes
place sounds a monotonous rhythm offstage. As the pace of the
action accelerates, the tempo of the drum increases. Starting at
a normal pulse beat, it quickens imperceptibly, and by the end
of the performance the heartbeat of everyone present corre-
sponds to the now frenzied rhythm of the drum.

Two other plays written during this period were to employ
stage devices to supplement the action and "express" O'Neill's
meaning. Color symbolism is used most effectively in *All God's
Chillun* to present the problems confronting the parties to an
inter-racial marriage. And in *The Hairy Ape* a cage-like ship's
hold and mechanical, doll-like figures help to point out man's
plight in an over-mechanized world. But it was with *Anna
Christie,* a more conventional play of the sea, that O'Neill
won his second Pulitzer Prize in 1922. The play deals, rather
sentimentally, with a woman who is redeemed, under the influence of the sea and a man's love, from a life of degradation.
O'Neill, far from considering it one of his better plays, omitted
it from the representative volume of his work, *Nine Plays,*
published in 1932.

Desire Under the Elms (1924), though it won no prizes, is
one of O'Neill's great plays. A penetrating analysis of the main-

spring of Yankee character, all of its action takes place in or immediately outside of a New England farmhouse. It is a tremendously difficult play to produce, for, with various portions of the front wall removed, simultaneous action is revealed in different portions of the interior. Requiring highly skilful actors, the play failed miserably at its first staging. Admirers of O'Neill long had to content themselves with reading the play. Recently, however, it has been successfully revived on the stage, with Miss Carol Stone in the role of Abbie and a highly trained supporting cast.

During the years from 1925 to 1927 O'Neill and his family spent much time in Bermuda. Here the regimen of work and exercise continued. And the dramatic experimentation did not cease. Having expanded the stage through his use of rhythm, symbol, and simultaneous action, O'Neill attempted still other novel devices. *The Great God Brown,* written in 1926 under the influence of the psychoanalysts Freud and Jung, makes extensive use of masks in interpreting the split personality in man. By this time, however, O'Neill's experiments had been widely acclaimed. And when he produced the lengthy—nine act—*Strange Interlude* (1928), with its characters speaking their thoughts aloud upon the stage, the other actors pretending not to hear these speeches, he was awarded his third Pulitzer Prize.

Of course, O'Neill had had some failures. *The Fountain* (1925) is a poor play. And neither *Marco Millions* (1927) nor *Dynamo* (1929) is a great work of art. But he had also had much success. Three Pulitzer prizes in eight years is no mean feat. And it was not only popular recognition that O'Neill had achieved. He had produced at least one dramatic masterpiece. *Lazarus Laughed,* which O'Neill wrote in 1927, has been called "the supreme piece of drama of modern times." Compared with *Faust, Hamlet* and *Oedipus Rex,* it has been asserted by scholars that the play is "as complete a dramatic triumph as the theatre affords."

After over ten years of hard work, O'Neill felt the need for a change. He went abroad in 1928, visiting Europe and the Far East. Eventually he settled in a chateau near Tours, France. Here, after being divorced from his second wife, he married Carlotta Monterey, the actress. With his third wife for companion, O'Neill spent three years abroad, returning at the end of that time to build a new home, Casa Genotta, on Sea Island, Georgia.

When O'Neill came back to this country after his three-year absence, he had not only a new wife and a new home, but a new play as well. As a matter of fact, he had three plays. *Mourning Becomes Electra,* written in France and published here in 1931, is a trilogy, a "modern psychological drama using one of the old legend plots of Greek tragedy," as O'Neill tells us in his *Diary.* Set in New England at the time of the Civil War, the three parts of the play correspond to the three parts of Aeschylus' interpretation of the legend of Agamemnon upon which it is patterned. O'Neill's boldest and surest play, it deliberately challenges comparison with its great source. It has been maintained that it does not suffer through such a comparison. *Mourning Becomes Electra* is one of the great dramatic monuments of all times.

The two plays that followed O'Neill's great trilogy were failures. Though *Ah, Wilderness!* achieved some measure of popular success, it is a slight comedy. Written in a month between revisions of *Days Without End,* it is a quiet, nostalgic interlude in O'Neill's dramatic career. The latter play, the most contrived and melodramatic of O'Neill's works, is as dull on the stage as it is on the printed page. But the dramatist's earlier works had gained an international audience by this time. And in 1936 he was awarded the Nobel prize, the second American to be so honored.

The O'Neills left Sea Island for California in 1936. There, on a mountain top not far from Berkeley, they built another home, which they called Tao House. O'Neill had begun work on a series of plays that were to trace an American family through 150 years, beginning in 1775 and running through nine separate dramas. He had completed one play and spent over a year on preliminary plans for his great Cycle when, in 1937, he was stricken with a serious physical disorder. Years of sporadic attacks of illness followed, alternating with periods of comparative good health and intense dramatic activity. O'Neill withdrew from the world, writing and suffering on his mountain top. The plan of the Cycle was enlarged to make room for eleven dramas. Plays were written, revised, detached from the Cycle, destroyed. Other plays were completed and put aside, for O'Neill was unwilling to undergo the trial of production until he had a sizeable portion of the Cycle completed. Meanwhile, the attacks had increased in severity. The illness was diagnosed as Parkinson's disease, a disease affecting the use of the muscles by causing tremor and weakness. By 1946 the disease had so ravaged O'Neill's body that he was no longer able to write. When he was able to work at all, he had to resort to dictation.

Finally, his health somewhat improved, O'Neill emerged from retirement in 1946, coming to New York to supervise production of *The Iceman Cometh* and *A Moon for the Misbegotten*. Later the Theatre Guild was to do *A Touch of the Poet,* a Cycle play that O'Neill had detached and released for production as part of the loosely related group of plays then ready for rehearsal. These late plays were not very successful at the time. Critics said that O'Neill had been out of touch with the stage for too long a time. As a result, his plays were not theater but lengthy, talky, morbidly pessimistic expositions of his ideas. Though he had once been criticized for the amount of violence in his plays—12 murders, 8 suicides, 7 cases of insanity, and 23 more or less natural deaths are scattered through his earlier works—he was now condemned for morbidly contemplating life without producing any action. *The Iceman Cometh,* which the playwright had had great satisfaction in writing, was thought to be particularly defective in this respect.

The reception of O'Neill's latest work was a disappointment to him. Moreover, the strain and excitement of supervising the production of his plays proved exhausting. There were, in addition, publication details to be gone over, people to see, corrections to make. Knowing that his productive years were limited and anxious to get on with the enormous quantity of work he had outlined for himself, O'Neill was irritated by the drain on his energy. Quarrels with his wife, arising from his morose disposition and aggravated by the petulancy of sickness, became increasingly bitter. Other family problems added to his despair. His beautiful young daughter Oona married the elderly comedian Charlie Chaplin, despite her father's objections to the match. Shane, his youngest son, had developed into a confused and unmanageable young man. Finally came the shattering blow of his eldest son's suicide. Eugene O'Neill, Jr. had been a classics scholar and teacher at Yale. His articles and reviews were widely known, and his death came as a great shock to the learned world. His father was, of course, shaken by the news. And when, shortly after this event, his health failed again, he was forced to abandon work completely. He spent his few remaining years, a morose, bitter, lonely man, racked with pain, in solitude. He died in a Boston hotel on November 27, 1953.

Eugene O'Neill has emerged as one of America's greatest

tragic playwrights. One eminent critic of the theater has suggested the reason for it is that the mood of the people is just
right for introspection. *The Iceman Cometh* has been re-
evaluated and has returned to triumph over a theater that had
pampered and then neglected O'Neill. This play, as well as
Long Day's Journey into Night and *A Touch of the Poet*, show
how closely life and his plays overlapped, yet how brilliantly
he was able to impart art on reminiscence.

But regardless of what judgment his posthumously produced
works are afforded, his stature will remain great. He is the man
who, plunging into the American theater when it was nothing,
was able, in Lewis's words, "to transform it utterly . . . to a
world of splendor and fear and greatness." In doing so, he
created several plays that should live as long as there is a stage.

Stephen Vincent Benét

American muse, whose strong and diverse heart
So many men have tried to understand
But only made it smaller with their art,
Because you are as various as your land,

As mountainous—deep, as flowered with blue rivers,
Thirsty with deserts, buried under snows,
As native as the shape of Navajo quivers
And native, too, as the sea-voyaged rose.

Swift runner, never captured or subdued,
Seven-branched elk beside the mountain stream,
That half a hundred hunters have pursued
But never matched their bullets with the dream,

Where the great huntsmen failed, I set my sorry
And mortal snare for your immortal quarry.

WITH these words of invocation Stephen Vincent Benét
begins his famous poem of America and the Civil
War, *John Brown's Body*. Expressing as they do Benét's humility, his love of nature, his understanding of the variety that

is America, the lines might stand as an epigraph for all of the man's work. For as novelist, balladeer, story-teller, poet, and propagandist, Benét invoked the same muse to express his love for his country and the people who made it, and continue to make it, great. He is first and foremost a patriot. But his patriotism is not of that sentimental sort that is displayed in Fourth of July and campaign oratory. Nor is it of the hysterical stripe that extols America through indiscriminate attack, violating its principles while shouting its name. Benét's love for his country is deeper and truer. Immersed in its history, he can celebrate

> The prairie-schooner crawling toward the ore
> And the cheap car, parked by the station door.

And understanding its diversity, he can tolerate—indeed, rejoice in—its non-conformity.

Stephen Vincent Benét, interpreter of America, was born in Bethlehem, Pennsylvania, on July 22, 1898, the year of the Spanish-American war. The poet's great-great-grandfather had been Spanish. A Catalonian, he had entered the Spanish Merchant Marine. After several voyages, he settled in St. Augustine, Florida, in 1785. Later his children moved westward to Kentucky. It was from this state that Stephen's grandfather, after whom he was named, had left for West Point. He served with distinction as an officer and in later years he turned to authorship, writing army texts and translating military history from the French.

Colonel J. Walker Benét, the father of the poet, was also a West Pointer. And he shared his parent's interest in literature. Loving poetry, he would, "at the drop of a hat, discuss the more abstruse bards, like Chivers and Beddoes, with a Major-General or a startled Bishop." He read poetry aloud, to the delight of his family. Stephen's brother William, a poet himself, says of his father, "He acquainted us with the best, and aroused our interest in how it was constructed. . . . His reading voice could crinkle your backbone, and made you astonishedly aware of nobility and heroism—a valuable innoculation." His library was as good as his voice, and the children had the benefit of both. It was, as a matter of fact, his father's old Rebellion Records and his *Battles and Leaders of the Civil War* that fired young Stephen's interest in history and led, ultimately, to *John Brown's Body*.

The poet's mother, Frances Neill (Rose) Benét, was a quiet understanding woman. Herself a descendant of an old Kentucky military family, she followed her soldier husband about the country from post to post, wherever duty called. When her third child was born, her husband was supervising a government war contract at the Bethlehem Iron Works, and the family was living in a rented house on Fountain Hill in South Bethlehem. But before Stephen was out of his carriage, they had moved to Buffalo, New York. And when he was still wearing the "long golden curls" of babyhood, Stephen accompanied his mother, father, brother, and sister to a new post at the Watervleit Arsenal, between Albany and Troy, New York. Here he acquired the nickname "Tibbie" and a Cockney accent, which he picked up from his new, raspy-voiced English nurse. It was here, too, that he was discovered in the nursery one day, solemnly "reading" from an upside down book to a dead mouse in a trap.

Since army officers never stay long in one place, the family had moved again by the time the boy was of school age. This time it was to an ordnance arsenal clear across the country, in Benicia, California. Here young Stephen had a donkey and a two-wheeled cart to ride in. Unfortunately, the donkey was as uncooperative as that species of beast often is, and as soon as anyone would get into the cart, the donkey would lie down in the road. There was also a curly brown dog named Prince, a sleepy and, according to an elderly aunt who lived with the family, a smelly animal. But eight-year-old Stephen would hear no criticism of the dog, who was at this period his constant companion.

Though Stephen went on occasional jaunts with his brother, who was twelve years older than he, games and sports held little interest for him. A frail, rather delicate child, he preferred reading to athletics. In addition to *Peck's Bad Boy*, the Henty books, Dumas, Lang, and "E. Nesbit," he read more serious books. Howard Pyle's *Men of Iron* and William Morris's prose and poetry were special favorites, and from such books "he began to gain an idea of how the past could be presented in terms of realistic detail." However, the boy soon developed a chronic nearsightedness from "constant reading in any dim corner." Peering out from behind his rimless spectacles, the serious-looking youngster suggests, in an early drawing by his brother, "the Supreme Court about to come to a decision."

Such a serious, bookish boy was not very popular with his fellow students when, at the age of about ten, he was sent to the Hitchcock Military Academy. He did not care for the school, and his indignation at the brutality of the boys is reflected in his later poem about Shelley at Eton:

> Round about
> Struggled a howling crowd of boys, pell-mell,
> Pushing and jostling like a stormy sea,
> With shouting faces turned a pasty white
> By the strange light, for foam. They all had clods,
> Or slimy balls of mud. A few gripped stones.
> And there, his back against the battered door,
> His pile of books scattered about his feet,
> Stood Shelley while two others held him fast,
> And the clods beat upon him.

But at home Stephen was indulged, being allowed, according to his brother, many more privileges than had attended his own early years. Indeed, his father "developed a liking for controversy" with the small boy. And his brother remembered Stephen best "reclining upon the back of his neck in a certain large familiar leather armchair drawling his 'maybe so, but—' to some argument of my father's, who sat across from him beyond the book-laden table."

It was while living in the big house near San Francisco Bay in California that Stephen first began to write. "There were," says his brother, "early stories . . . composed while the author absorbed some horrifying concoction of a strange and lurid color which he got together in the kitchen from God knows what ingredients!" There were poems, too. And when he was just thirteen, Stephen won a cash prize from the *Saint Nicholas League* with a short poem called *The Regret of Dives.*

Shortly after Stephen won his first prize for poetry, the family moved again. Indeed, the young prize-winner spent his prize money on the train coming east to Augusta, Georgia, where his father had been assigned a new post. Stephen missed the companionship of his brother in the new house in Georgia, for William had become a publisher's reader in New York by this time. But he was happier in his new school, where he completed his secondary education. And he still had books for companions. He had already discovered that poetry "was not a dead thing or an alien thing or a dry game of words. . . . I knew it was always written by the living," he says, "even though the date-line said that the man was dead." At the age of 17, he published his own first book of poetry.

World War I was threatening when Benét left Georgia for Yale. His interests at college were primarily literary and, in company with Thornton Wilder, Archibald MacLeish and

Philip Barry, he was soon on the staff of the *Yale Literary Magazine*. Later he became chairman of the *Lit*. And in his junior year a poem which he wrote about Keats was chosen as the University Prize Poem.

In the meantime, war had erupted and the United States had been drawn into it. Benét enlisted in the army, but his defective vision caused him to be rejected almost at once. He left college for a war-time job in the State Department. Rooming in Washington with his college chum Thornton Wilder, he worked as a cipher-clerk in the same department as James Thurber, an artist with eyesight as poor as his own.

When the war ended, Benét returned to Yale for his B.A. While there the University Press published *Young Adventure*, a book of poems that he had worked on while in Washington. Upon graduation, Benét worked briefly for a New York advertising firm, but he soon tired of the work and decided to devote his life to literature. He returned to Yale for another year's work and a master's degree, presenting in lieu of a thesis his third book of poems, *Heavens and Earth*.

Benét spent the summer after he received his master's degree writing his first novel, *The Beginning of Wisdom*. When he had completed it, he went abroad for further study. While living a somewhat bohemian life and studying at the Sorbonne, he met a pretty, talented, young American girl who was writing for the Paris edition of the Chicago *Tribune* and covering Paris for the London *Daily Mail*. Her name was Rosemary Carr, and Steve Benét was soon in love with her. They returned to Chicago, the girl's home town, for their marriage. And while plans for the wedding were under way, the anxious young bridegroom turned out another novel, *Young People's Pride*. The book was serialized in *Harper's Bazaar*, and the income it provided enabled the young couple to return to France for the early months of their marriage. His new bride loved

Paris, and in a later poem, *Little Testament,* Benét tells us of his

Loving two countries well, sweet France, like a well-sunned pear
And this red, hard apple, America, tart flavored, tasting of the
    wild.

Back in New York, Benét published another novel, *Jean Huguenot.* Then he turned to the short story, writing for the magazines until his powers of invention began to run thin. With his stories getting flimsier and flimsier, he decided that a complete break-away was necessary. Ever since he had first read his father's military records in the library of the house in Benicia, he had contemplated a long narrative poem on the American Civil War. In 1926 he applied to the Guggenheim Foundation for a fellowship, outlining his plan for the poem. Winning the fellowship, he took his wife and young daughter abroad with him, anxious to work without distraction and stretch the modest stipend as far as it would go. At Neuilly, he began work, carrying home huge piles of books from the Paris libraries to help re-create the Civil War background. The work came hard at first, for his only experience in welding historical materials into an artistic whole had been in a novel of Florida called *Spanish Bayonet,* which he had published just before he left America. But his "long armchair discussions with his father, in California and Georgia" came back to him vividly and inspired him to go on. When the book was eventually published, in 1928, it became a best-seller overnight. The following year it was awarded the Pulitzer prize. Sceptical friends and relatives had thought Benét extravagant and insane when, with a wife and daughter to support, he had given up magazine writing to work on a book "that had to be written." Now they were willing to concede that the gamble had paid off.

With the acclaim of critics and public ringing in his ears, Benét no longer had to grind out stories to pay his bills. He could set his own pace. And his work improved as a result. Before he started any new work, however, Benét published a collection of ballads and poems that he had written over a period of fifteen years. In it he celebrates American names and people. The names are:

> The sharp names that never get fat,
> The snakeskin-titles of mining-claims,
> The plumed war-bonnet of Medicine Hat,
> Tucson and Deadwood and Lost Mule Flat.

The people are men like William Sycamore, whose

> . . . father, he was a mountaineer
> His fist was a knotty hammer,

And Hill-Billy Jim, who plays all night and wins the great fiddler's prize. And anyone who can match the tricky rhythms of "The Mountain Whippoorwill" "—well, he's got to fiddle hard."

Benét also collaborated with his wife on a book of rhymes about historic Americans for children. Another novel, *James Shore's Daughter*, followed in 1933. When Benét returned to the short story, he did so with renewed vigor. *Thirteen O'Clock* was published in 1937. This collection includes one of Benét's best stories, a story that has already become a minor American classic, appearing in every anthology of American short stories as well as on the screen and, set to music, as a light opera. I am referring, of course, to *The Devil and Daniel Webster*. It is a fantastic story and a delightful one. For Dan'l, who "never left a jug or a case half finished" in his life, takes on the case of Jabez Stone and finds himself pleading before a jury of resurrected fiends. With Satan as the opposing lawyer, Dan'l has need of all his New Hampshire wits before the trial is over.

Benét had always been a devotee of the pulp magazines of horror, mystery, and marvel. Now he showed himself a master of the fantastic with such stories as *Johnny Pye and the Fool Killer* and *Doc Mellhorn and the Pearly Gates*. And in verse too he exploited this vein. *Metropolitan Nightmare,* for instance, is an eerie poem about "the year the termites came to New York." But he was doing other things as well. He wrote an operetta for radio called *The Headless Horseman,* based on Washington Irving's *Legend of Sleepy Hollow*. He collaborated with Douglas Moore, the musician, on *Power and the Land,* a film for the the Rural Electrification Administration. In addition to work for radio and the films, he joined the staff of the *Saturday Review of Literature,* one of America's most popular literary reviews. As editor of the Yale Series of Younger Poets, he assisted many aspiring young artists, including the important young poet, Muriel Rukeyser.

With all this work, there was still time for his family. He had two daughters now, and a son. With them, he divided his time between the large house in the old whaling port of Stonington, Connecticut and a New York apartment. In New York he shared his air-conditioned study with his wife, who did translations of the French novels of Colette, reviewed children's books, and collaborated with her husband on a series of thumbnail biographies of writers.

The years had brought recognition to Benét, and in addition to the two homes and the air-conditioned study, there were other less material rewards. He was elected Vice President of the National Institute of Arts and Letters. Membership in the American Academy was bestowed upon him. He won the Roosevelt Medal and the O. Henry Story Prize. Indeed, his brother William, himself a Pulitzer prize winner, complained with friendly envy about Steve's ability to win prizes. "Every time they put one up," he said, "they decide to give it to him!"

Life, however, was not all happiness, prizes and success. There were trials, too, for the tall, dark, balding, bespectacled writer. His vision was extremely poor and his eyes troubled him occasionally. Moreover, he suffered for years with the excruciating pain of arthritis. But more troublesome than his personal afflictions was the knowledge that good people everywhere were suffering needlessly. His brother's son, James, had spent two years as an ambulance driver with the Spanish Loyalists. Through him, Benét had first-hand accounts of the horrors of war and oppression. And he could see those twin spectres rising in country after country. Much of his time was spent in warning and exhortation. With the onset of World War II, he gave unsparingly of his time and energy in the cause of freedom. *They Burned the Books* and *Listen to the People* were two of his most successful counter-blasts to the propaganda of the dictators. And in letters, speeches, articles and broadcasts he fought the battle of freedom as surely as the men in the front lines.

Benét's war-time activity left him little freedom for his art. But he had long contemplated a narrative poem about the American frontier. He had started it in 1934, and it had been laid aside and taken up again at odd intervals over the years. By 1943 he had completed the first book of a projected five. He called it *Western Star*, and it was ready for publication when, suddenly, on March 13, 1943, he was stricken with a heart attack and died instantly. On his desk at the time of his grievous death were notes for the continuation of *Western*

Star. Among the last things that he had written was a typical bit of verse:

> Now for my country that it still may live,
> All that I have, all that I am I'll give.
> It is not much beside the gift of the brave
> And yet accept it since tis all I have.

Index